A
POEM
FOR
EVERY
AUTUMN
DAY

EDITED BY ALLIE ESIRI

Also edited by Allie Esiri
from Macmillan

A Poem for Every Night of the Year

A Poem for Every Day of the Year

Shakespeare for Every Day of the Year

A POEM FOR EVERY AUTUMN DAY

EDITED BY ALLIE ESIRI

MACMILLAN

Published 2020 by Macmillan Children's Books
an imprint of Pan Macmillan
The Smithson, 6 Briset Street, London EC1M 5NR
EU representative: Macmillan Publishers Ireland Ltd, 1st Floor,
The Liffey Trust Centre, 117-126 Sheriff Street Upper,
Dublin 1, DO1 YC43
Associated companies throughout the world
www.panmacmillan.com

ISBN 978-1-5290-4522-2

This collection copyright © Allie Esiri 2020
All poems copyright © the individual poets

The right of Allie Esiri to be identified as the editor
of this work has been asserted by her in accordance
with the Copyright, Designs and Patents Act 1988.

All rights reserved. No part of this publication may be reproduced,
stored in a retrieval system, or transmitted, in any form or by any means
(electronic, mechanical, photocopying, recording or otherwise),
without the prior written permission of the publisher.

Pan Macmillan does not have any control over, or any responsibility for,
any author or third-party websites referred to in or on this book.

3 5 7 9 8 6 4

A CIP catalogue record for this book is available from the British Library.

Printed and bound by CPI Group (UK) Ltd, Croydon CR0 4YY

MIX
Paper from
responsible sources
FSC® C116313

This book is sold subject to the condition that it shall not,
by way of trade or otherwise, be lent, resold, hired out,
or otherwise circulated without the publisher's prior consent
in any form of binding or cover other than that in which
it is published and without a similar condition including this
condition being imposed on the subsequent purchaser.

For Jack Esiri

Contents

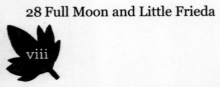

October

xiii

Introduction

Within the pages of this anthology, one of a four-part cycle of seasons, you will find some of the finest poetry ever to have been written about Autumn – with all its vitality and variety – and the key cultural and historical events that lie amidst the dates of September, October and November.

However, the title of this collection is something of a misnomer. Each day of autumn hosts not just one poem, but two, almost all of which have been drawn from my earlier anthologies: *A Poem for Every Day of the Year* and *A Poem for Every Night of the Year*. The idea is to provide you with a poem for each Autumn morning, through which you can shape your perception of your day, as well as another to help you unwind and reflect in the evening.

Presenting two poems tailored for opposite ends of your day seems particularly fitting for an anthology devoted to Autumn, a season characterised by its sense of harmonious equilibrium between different states of being. It marries the lingering heat and brightness of the waning summer with the cold and creeping darkness of the forthcoming winter. It is a time in which things draw to a close. Leaves fall and die in fiery heaps and animals (and humans) prepare to retreat from sunny meadows and hillsides into cosier, confined spaces away from the elements. Yet it is also defined by an upsurge of life, renewal and abundance. Crops are harvested and enjoyed after months of anticipation, while children and students

xv

begin their new scholarly adventures, often waved off by a relative in the autumn of their years. Balance is to be found at every autumnal juncture. Well, it is the season of Libra after all.

These pages contain poems that capture every one of these gently conflicting features of Autumn – beginning with Gerard Manley Hopkins's stirring pastoral celebration 'Hurrahing In Harvest' and closing with Robert Frost's elegiac and sobering 'Nothing Gold Can Stay'. There is, of course, a significant emphasis throughout this anthology on pastoral life; lines written to share and preserve the fleeting, beautiful transitional moments such as Rachel Field's 'Something Told the Wild Geese' or tributes to the enduring majesty of nature in the midst of all this flux, as in Walt Whitman's 'Song of Myself'.

Some texts offer us just a photograph-like snapshot of a time and place, like 'The Red Wheelbarrow' by William Carlos Williams, while others, such as great poet of the natural world John Clare, provide us with a stream of images with as much movement as a modern day film, as in 'Pleasant Sounds'. And then there's Oscar Wilde and Eleanor Farjeon, whose poetry takes from the practices of visual art using the literary device known as 'ekphrasis'. William Wordsworth summed up the relationship between words and images evocatively when he wrote, 'We are fond of tracing the resemblance between Poetry and Painting, and, accordingly, we call them Sisters'.

It will come as no surprise when you come across the most famous lines ever written about the season in John Keats' stunningly immersive and dreamlike 1819 ode, 'To Autumn' – near the anthology's midway point. Although it provides a beautiful evocation of the natural world, it is also steeped in a topical context, referring obliquely, though unmistakably, to the Peterloo Massacre of August 1819. The structure of this anthology is inspired by poems like this, melding the characteristics of the season with social history.

Alongside poems about the time of year, you will find texts that shed light on significant autumnal dates. November is filled with works by the War Poets, with the early works imbued with sunny, patriotic optimism, and the later texts laced with the horrors of war and the bitter disillusionment of the young soldiers. Elsewhere, the 1415 Battle of Agincourt is marked by extracts from Shakespeare's Henry V, and the American Civil War is approached, not through a traditional poem, but through the poetry of Abraham Lincoln's words in his rousing Gettysburg Address.

Short introductions to each piece will provide some crucial bits of context, but the poetry itself can often be more powerful than the cold facts when it comes to conveying what a moment in history was really like. But this book doesn't only look at the distant past; recent, era-defining autumn events such as 9/11 are remembered, in amongst centuries-old traditions such as All Hallows Eve or St Andrew's Day.

By the same token, the texts in this anthology have been chosen so that modern and contemporary luminaries can be given a platform alongside all the canonical greats who too often dominate these kinds of books. Diversity and a plurality of voices are at the heart of this collection which seeks to champion long-overlooked female doyennes such as Amy Lowell and Adelaide Crapsey, as well as global superstars from across the ages from Rumi to Rabindranath Tagore to Nikki Giovanni.

Although the seasons provide us with common

ground and shared experience, every writer has their own interpretation of their time and surroundings. Here you will find an array of texts that give deeply personal perspectives, from 'Crab-Apples' by Imtiaz Dharker, in which the poet reaches backwards towards her childhood in her native Pakistan, to Seamus Heaney's 'Digging' which builds a bridge between the writer and his father and grandfather. And then there are the literary renegades who challenge conventions of form and language to develop their own singular style, such as E.E. Cummings whose ingenious 'l(a' recreates the falling of a leaf through its setting on the printed page.

That poem explicitly addresses the loneliness that can emerge within us as the days shorten, and the darkness encroaches. *A Poem For Every Autumn Day* not only salutes the joys of Autumn, but offers poems of consolation that will speak to you on a damp, grey morning, or comfort you through a dark night. Here you have a trusty companion for life – one that will always be there, to awaken your spirit, question, console and sustain you from every 1 September to 30 November. After that, fear not – *A Poem for Every Winter Day* will be on hand for when December comes around.

Allie Esiri

September

1 September · Hurrahing in Harvest · Gerard Manley Hopkins

In this vibrant and vital poem, Gerard Manley Hopkins recreates the overwhelming joy he felt on one particular autumnal stroll, and, through the immediacy of his verse, lets us share in his awe for this bucolic harvest scene. There are clear religious overtones, but these lines also offer a celebration of the unpredictable, wild wonders of nature in autumn.

Summer ends now; now, barbarous in beauty, the
  stooks arise
  Around; up above, what wind-walks! what lovely
  behaviour
  Of silk-sack clouds! has wilder, wilful-wavier
Meal-drift moulded ever and melted across skies?

I walk, I lift up, I lift up heart, eyes,
  Down all that glory in the heavens to glean our Saviour;
  And eyes, heart, what looks, what lips yet give you a
Rapturous love's greeting of realer, of rounder replies?

And the azurous hung hills are his world-wielding
    shoulder
  Majestic — as a stallion stalwart, very-violet-sweet! —
These things, these things were here and but the beholder
  Wanting; which two when they once meet,
The heart rears wings bold and bolder
  And hurls for him, O half hurls earth for him off under
    his feet.

☾ 1 September · Aeroplanes · Herbert Read

On 1 September 1939, Germany invaded Poland.
The Allied Powers had vowed to help Poland if it was
attacked, and so, two days later, Britain, France and
members of the Commonwealth declared war on
Germany, marking the beginning of World War Two.
The war would last for almost exactly six years, and
ended on 2 September 1945. Herbert Read's interests in
nature and war meet in this poem which was published
in 1966.

A dragonfly
in a flecked grey sky.

Its silvered planes
break the wide and still
harmony of space.

Around it shells
flash
their fumes
burgeoning to blooms
smoke-liles that float
along the sky.

Among them darts
a dragonfly.

2 September · But I Can't · W. H. Auden

Written in 1940, this poem expresses the uncertainties of
everyday life in wartime. Not only is the future unknown,
but the reasoning behind the war seems as uncertain as
the source of the wind. The poem takes the unusual form
of a villanelle – a poem formed of five tercets followed by
a final quatrain, with two rhymes and two refrains.

Time will say nothing but I told you so,
Time only knows the price we have to pay;
If I could tell you I would let you know.

If we should weep when clowns put on their show,
If we should stumble when musicians play,
Time will say nothing but I told you so.

There are no fortunes to be told, although,
Because I love you more than I can say,
If I could tell you I would let you know.

The winds must come from somewhere when they blow,
There must be reason why the leaves decay;
Time will say nothing but I told you so.

Perhaps the roses really want to grow,
The vision seriously intends to stay;
If I could tell you I would let you know.

Suppose the lions all get up and go,
And the brooks and soldiers run away;
Will Time say nothing but I told you so?
If I could tell you I would let you know.

5

In between the First and Second World Wars, the British town of Slough in Berkshire was used as a dumping ground for war surplus materials, before becoming a site of manufacturing and home to over 850 new factories. John Betjeman wrote this poem in 1937, lamenting the onset of industrialization.

Come, friendly bombs, and fall on Slough
It isn't fit for humans now,
There isn't grass to graze a cow
    Swarm over, Death!

Come, bombs, and blow to smithereens
Those air-conditioned, bright canteens,
Tinned fruit, tinned meat, tinned milk, tinned beans,
    Tinned minds, tinned breath.

Mess up the mess they call a town—
A house for ninety-seven down
And once a week a half-a-crown
    For twenty years.

And get that man with double chin
Who'll always cheat and always win,
Who washes his repulsive skin
    In women's tears,

And smash his desk of polished oak
And smash his hands so used to stroke
And stop his boring dirty joke
    And make him yell.

But spare the bald young clerks who add
The profits of the stinking cad;
It's not their fault that they are mad,
    They've tasted Hell.

It's not their fault they do not know
The birdsong from the radio,
It's not their fault they often go
    To Maidenhead

And talk of sport and makes of cars
In various bogus-Tudor bars
And daren't look up and see the stars
    But belch instead.

In labour-saving homes, with care
Their wives frizz out peroxide hair
And dry it in synthetic air
    And paint their nails.

Come, friendly bombs, and fall on Slough
To get it ready for the plough.
The cabbages are coming now;
    The earth exhales.

3 September · Composed Upon Westminster Bridge, September 3, 1802 · William Wordsworth

This poem describes London and the River Thames, viewed from Westminster Bridge in the early morning. Wordsworth was travelling to Calais with his sister Dorothy at the time, and in her journal, Dorothy wrote this of the sight: 'Yet the sun shone so brightly with such a pure light that there was even something like the purity of one of nature's own grand Spectacles.'

Earth has not anything to show more fair:
Dull would he be of soul who could pass by
A sight so touching in its majesty:
This City now doth, like a garment, wear
The beauty of the morning; silent, bare,
Ships, towers, domes, theatres, and temples lie
Open unto the fields, and to the sky;
All bright and glittering in the smokeless air.
Never did sun more beautifully steep
In his first splendour, valley, rock, or hill;
Ne'er saw I, never felt, a calm so deep!
The river glideth at his own sweet will:
Dear God! the very houses seem asleep;
And all that mighty heart is lying still!

☾ 3 September · This is the House That Jack Built · Anon.

'This is the House That Jack Built' is a popular nursery rhyme, the origins of which most likely lie in the sixteenth century. It is often sung as a 'cumulative poem', meaning that the line 'That lay in the house that Jack built' is repeated after each new line before the song begins again – so that the poem unfolds into a more and more complex structure: like the building of a house.

This is the farmer sowing his corn,
That kept the cock that crowed in the morn,
That waked the priest all shaven and shorn,
That married the man all tattered and torn,
That kissed the maiden all forlorn,
That milked the cow with the crumpled horn,
That tossed the dog,
That worried the cat,
That killed the rat,
That ate the malt
That lay in the house that Jack built.

4 September · The Solitary Reaper · William Wordsworth

In this poem, Wordsworth's speaker describes the experience of seeing a girl singing in a field as she reaps, cutting and binding the grain. Wordsworth speculates about what kind of song the girl could be singing.

Behold her, single in the field,
Yon solitary Highland Lass!
Reaping and singing by herself;
Stop here, or gently pass!
Alone she cuts and binds the grain,
And sings a melancholy strain;
O listen! for the Vale profound
Is overflowing with the sound.

No Nightingale did ever chaunt
More welcome notes to weary bands
Of travellers in some shady haunt,
Among Arabian sands:
A voice so thrilling ne'er was heard
In spring-time from the Cuckoo-bird,
Breaking the silence of the seas
Among the farthest Hebrides.

Will no one tell me what she sings?
Perhaps the plaintive numbers flow
For old, unhappy, far-off things,
And battles long ago:
Or is it some more humble lay,
Familiar matter of today?
Some natural sorrow, loss, or pain,
That has been, and may be again?

Whate'er the theme, the Maiden sang
As if her song could have no ending;
I saw her singing at her work,
And o'er the sickle bending;—
I listened, motionless and still;
And, as I mounted up the hill,
The music in my heart I bore,
Long after it was heard no more.

☾ 4 September · Hornbeacon High ·
Sarah Crossan

The start of September and the end of the Summer
Holidays mean one thing to schoolchildren across the
country – a thing that fills some hearts with terror: Back
To School. This poem about school is actually an extract
from a verse novel called *One*. It tells the story of two
sisters who are conjoined twins.

The building is white,
ivy eating its way up the broken walls,
windows small
and scratched.

Most students are
pulling at one another and squealing,
basking in their easy friendly reunions.

But I
study those
who are alone,
at the edge of this noise,
the kids holding their school bags close,
keeping their eyes down,

so I can
impersonate their
invisibility.

☀ **5 September** · Please Mrs Butler · Allan Ahlberg

This poem by the children's writer Allan Ahlberg is a comical story about life in the classroom – it is not just the children who get fed up with being interrogated!

Please Mrs Butler
This boy Derek Drew
Keeps copying my work, Miss.
What shall I do?

Go and sit in the hall, dear.
Go and sit in the sink.
Take your books on the roof, my lamb.
Do whatever you think.

Please Mrs Butler
This boy Derek Drew
Keeps taking my rubber, Miss.
What shall I do?

Keep it in your hand, dear.
Hide it up your vest.
Swallow it if you like, love.
Do what you think best.

13

Please Mrs Butler
This boy Derek Drew
Keeps calling me rude names, Miss.
What shall I do?

Lock yourself in the cupboard, dear.
Run away to sea.
Do whatever you can, my flower.
But *don't ask me!*

5 September · Ring a Ring o' Roses · Anon.

This song is a nursery rhyme which was first printed in England in 1881. There are many versions of this rhyme, including some that originate in Germany, Switzerland and the Netherlands. Some people believe that the rhyme dates from the Great Plague in 1665, or earlier breakouts of the Black Death, and that the lyrics describe the symptoms of the disease. From 2–6 September 1666 the Great Fire of London raged through the city, destroying many of the buildings and – perhaps – the plague along with it.

Ring a ring o' roses,
A pocket full of posies,
A-tishoo! A-tishoo!
We all fall down.

6 September · Homework! Oh, Homework! · Jack Prelutsky

Although there are some exciting things about the beginning of term, this poem takes as its subject something that many students dread: homework!

Homework! Oh, Homework!
I hate you! You stink!
I wish I could wash you away in the sink, if only a bomb
would explode you to bits.
Homework! Oh, homework!
You're giving me fits.

I'd rather take baths
with a man-eating shark, or wrestle a lion
alone in the dark,
eat spinach and liver,
pet ten porcupines,
than tackle the homework my teacher assigns.

Homework! Oh, homework! You're last on my list,
I simply can't see
why you even exist,

if you just disappeared
it would tickle me pink. Homework! Oh, homework!
    I hate you! You stink!

6 September · Reading the Classics ·
Brian Patten

A bedtime story, if well told, can last a lifetime or
longer. Brian Patten's poem pays homage to great works
of children's literature that continue to give, and to live
a life of their own.

The Secret Garden will never age;
The tangled undergrowth remains as fresh
As when the author put down her pen.
Its mysteries are as poignant now as then.

Though Time's a thief it cannot thieve
One page from the world of make-believe.

On the track the Railway Children wait;
Alice still goes back and forth through the glass;
In Tom's Midnight Garden Time unfurls,
And children still discover secret worlds.

At the Gates of Dawn Pan plays his pipes;
Mole and Ratty still float in awe downstream.
The weasels watch, hidden in the grass.
None cares how quickly human years pass.

Though Time's a thief it cannot thieve
One page from the world of make-believe.

✹ 7 September · The Lesson ·
Edward Lucie-Smith

Anyone who has ever lost a loved one will know that
grief is a complex emotion. Sometimes, consolation can
come in the form of merely knowing that grief, even
in its strangest forms, is a normal part of dealing with
loss. In this remarkable poem by Edward Lucie-Smith,
grief carries with it guilt, shame, relief, shock, and even
pride.

'Your father's gone,' my bald headmaster said.
His shiny dome and brown tobacco jar
Splintered at once in tears. It wasn't grief.
I cried for knowledge which was bitterer
Than any grief. For there and then I knew
That grief has uses – that a father dead
Could bind the bully's fist a week or two;
And then I cried for shame, then for relief.

I was a month past ten when I learnt this:
I still remember how the noise was stilled
in school-assembly when my grief came in.
Some goldfish in a bowl quietly sculled
Around their shining prison on its shelf.
They were indifferent. All the other eyes
Were turned towards me. Somewhere in myself
Pride, like a goldfish, flashed a sudden fin.

7 September · Talk Us Through It, Charlotte · Allan Ahlberg

Allan Ahlberg has written over twenty books for children over the course of his career, many of which were illustrated by his wife, Janet. You might know some of them, such as *The Jolly Postman* and *Each Peach Pear Plum*. The heroine of this poem outplays all of the boys on the field.

Well I shouldn't've been playin' really
Only there to watch me brother
My friend fancies his friend, y'know.
Anyway they was a man short.

Stay out on the wing, they said
Give 'em something to think about.
So I did that for about an hour;
Never passed to me or anything.

The ball kind of rebounded to me.
I thought, I'll have a little run with it.
I mean, they wasn't passin' to me
Was they? So off I went.

I ran past the first boy
He sort of fell over.
It was a bit slippery on that grass
I will say that for him.

19

Two more of 'em come at me
Only they sort of tackled each other
Collided – arh. I kept going.
There was this great big fat boy.

One way or another I kicked it
Through his legs and run round him.
That took a time. Me brother
Was shouting, Pass it to me, like.

Well like I said, I'd been there an hour.
They never give *me* a pass
Never even spoke to me
Or anything. So I kept going.

Beat this other boy somehow
Then there was just the goalie.
Out he came, spreadin' himself
As they say. I was really worried.

I thought he was going to hug me.
So I dipped me shoulder like they do
And the goalie moved one way, y'know
And I slammed it in the net.

Turned out afterwards it was the winner.
The manager said I was very good.
He wants me down at trainin' on Tuesday.
My friend says she's comin' as well.

8 September · An Attempt at Unrhymed Verse · Wendy Cope

Modern poets often turn away from rhyme schemes and from metre, preferring free verse. But in this amusing poem by Wendy Cope, the freedom of free verse proves a stretch too far for the poet, and she cannot quite shake her compulsion to think in rhymes.

People tell you all the time,
Poems do not have to rhyme.
It's often better if they don't
And I'm determined this one won't.
                              Oh dear.

Never mind, I'll start again.
Busy, busy with my pen . . . cil.
I can do it if I try –
Easy, peasy, pudding and gherkins.

Writing verse is so much fun,
Cheering as the summer weather,
Makes you feel alert and bright,
'Specially when you get it more or less the way you
      want it.

'Arithmetic' is the name for the part of Maths that deals with addition, subtraction, multiplication and division. Can you work any of these sums out?

Arithmetic is where numbers fly like pigeons in and out of your head.
Arithmetic tells you how many you lose or win if you know how many you had before you lost or won.
Arithmetic is seven eleven all good children go to heaven — or five six bundle of sticks.
Arithmetic is numbers you squeeze from your head to your hand to your pencil to your paper till you get the answer.
Arithmetic is where the answer is right and everything is nice and you can look out of the window and see the blue sky — or the answer is wrong and you have to start all over and try again and see how it comes out this time.
If you take a number and double it and double it again and then
double it a few more times, the number gets bigger and bigger
and goes higher and higher and only arithmetic can tell you
what the number is when you decide to quit doubling.
Arithmetic is where you have to multiply — and you carry the
multiplication table in your head and hope you won't lose it.

If you have two animal crackers, one good and one bad,
  and you
    eat one and a striped zebra with streaks all over him
    eats the
    other, how many animal crackers will you have if
    somebody
    offers you five six seven and you say No no no and
    you say
    Nay nay nay and you say Nix nix nix?
If you ask your mother for one fried egg for breakfast
  and she
    gives you two fried eggs and you eat both of them,
    who is
    better in arithmetic, you or your mother?

Since earliest times, poetry was celebrated as a great gift of memory; the ancient Greeks even invoked the goddess Mnemosyne, meaning 'memory', at the start of their poems. We usually write words down or else we store them in our computers, but sometimes it is good to memorize a poem; that way, we truly own it, and can carry its words with us always.

Why not take a poem
wherever you go?
pop it in your pocket
nobody will know

Take it to your classroom
stick it on the wall
tell them all about it
read it in the hall

Take it to the bathroom
tuck it up in bed
take the time to learn it
keep it in your head

take it for a day trip
take it on a train
fold it as a hat
when it starts to rain

Take it to a river
fold it as a boat
pop it in the water
hope that it will float

Take it to a hilltop
fold it as a plane
throw it up skywards
   time and time again

Take it to a post box
send it anywhere
out into the world with
tender
      loving
         care

☾ 9 September · The Hurt Boy and the Birds · John Agard

This poem takes bullying as its subject. Unable to talk to humans, the boy in this poem finds strength and inspiration through talking to birds.

The hurt boy talked to the birds
and fed them the crumbs of his heart.

It was not easy to find the words
for secrets he hid under his skin.
The hurt boy spoke of a bully's fist
that made his face a bruised moon –
his spectacles stamped to ruin.

It was not easy to find the words
for things that nightly hissed
as if his pillow was a hideaway for creepy-crawlies –
the note sent to the girl he fancied
held high in mockery.

But the hurt boy talked to the birds
and their feathers gave him welcome –

Their wings taught him new ways to become.

10 September · Pleasant Sounds · John Clare

It might be said that many of the great nature poets are in some respects compilers of lists – cataloguers of flowers and trees and animals. Perhaps something of the sort crossed Clare's mind when he sat down to write 'Pleasant Sounds', which is a poem in the form of a list of autumn images which cleverly captures a sense of the sound of nature.

The rustling of leaves under the feet in woods and under
    hedges;
The crumping of cat-ice and snow down wood-rides,
    narrow lanes, and every street causeway;
Rustling through a wood or rather rushing, while the
    wind halloos in the oak-toop like thunder;
The rustle of birds' wings startled from their nests or
    flying unseen into the bushes;
The whizzing of larger birds overhead in a wood, such as
    crows, puddocks, buzzards;
The trample of robins and woodlarks on the brown
    leaves, and the patter of squirrels on the green moss;
The fall of an acorn on the ground, the pattering of nuts
    on the hazel branches as they fall from ripeness;
The flirt of the groundlark's wing from the stubbles –
    how sweet such pictures on dewy mornings, when the
    dew flashes from its brown feathers.

☾ 10 September · Symphony in Yellow · Oscar Wilde

Oscar Wilde is best known for his acerbically witty plays, philosophical essays, and gently heartbreaking short stories, but he was also an accomplished poet. In this short piece from 1889 he describes an autumnal view from London's Embankment in which common features of the urban landscape – a bus, a barge, industrial smog – are reimagined as part of a natural world of butterflies and midges. The title may refer to music, but the effect of Wilde's verse, full of movement, atmosphere and vibrant colour seems to be more indebted to the paintings by his Impressionist contemporaries.

> An omnibus across the bridge
>   Crawls like a yellow butterfly,
>   And, here and there, a passer-by
> Shows like a little restless midge.
>
> Big barges full of yellow hay
>   Are moored against the shadowy wharf,
>   And, like a yellow silken scarf,
> The thick fog hangs along the quay.
>
> The yellow leaves begin to fade
>   And flutter from the Temple elms,
>   And at my feet the pale green Thames
> Lies like a rod of rippled jade.

11 September · The Right Word ·
Imtiaz Dharker

11 September marks one of the darkest days in recent history. On this day in 2001, terrorists hijacked four planes, and flew them towards targets in the United States. Two planes hit the World Trade Center in New York, and one flew into the Pentagon building in Washington; the fourth plane came down in a field after passengers tried to intervene. Imtiaz Dharker wrote this poem amid the public confusion following the attacks, when hostility was shown towards Middle Eastern people, and when the words 'freedom fighter' and 'terrorist' became highly contested labels.

Outside the door,
lurking in the shadows,
is a terrorist.

Is that the wrong description?
Outside that door,
taking shelter in the shadows,
is a freedom-fighter.

I haven't got this right.
Outside, waiting in the shadows
is a hostile militant.

29

Are words no more
than waving, wavering flags?
Outside your door,
watchful in the shadows,
is a guerrilla warrior.

God help me.
Outside, defying every shadow,
stands a martyr.
I saw his face.

No words can help me now.
Just outside the door,
lost in shadows,
is a child who looks like mine.

One word for you.
Outside my door,
his hand too steady,
his eyes too hard,
is a boy who looks like your son, too.

I open the door.
Come in, I say.
Come in and eat with us.

The child steps in
and carefully, at my door,
takes off his shoes.

11 September · The Convergence of the Twain · Simon Armitage

Thomas Hardy wrote a poem with this title to commemorate the sinking of the *Titanic* in 1912. Here, the poet Simon Armitage adopts Hardy's title and structure for his memorial to the events of 11 September 2011.

I

Here is an architecture of air.
Where dust has cleared,
nothing stands but free sky, unlimited and sheer.

II

Smoke's dark bruise
has paled, soothed
by wind, dabbed at and eased by rain, exposing the wound.

III

Over the spoil of junk,
rescuers prod and pick,
shout into tangled holes. What answers back is aftershock.

IV

All land lines are down.
Reports of mobile phones
are false. One half-excoriated Apple Mac still quotes the
    Dow Jones.

V

Shop windows are papered
with faces of the disappeared.
As if they might walk from the ruins – chosen, spared.

VI

With hindsight now we track
the vapour-trail of each flight-path
arcing through blue morning, like a curved thought.

VII

And in retrospect plot
the weird prospect
of a passenger plane beading an office-block.

VIII

But long before that dawn,
with those towers drawing
in worth and name to their full height, an opposite was
forming,

IX

a force
still years and miles off,
yet moving headlong forwards, locked on a collision
course.

X

Then time and space
contracted, so whatever distance
held those worlds apart thinned to an instant.

XI

During which, cameras framed
moments of grace
before the furious contact wherein earth and heaven
fused.

12 September · The Red Wheelbarrow · William Carlos Williams

This famous poem by William Carlos Williams is the perfect example of an 'imagist' poem, taking as its focal point a single snapshot of life. The poet's feelings and thoughts do not interfere with the act of observation. As a poem, it pushes the category of poetry itself to its limits.

so much depends
upon

a red wheel
barrow

glazed with rain
water

beside the white
chickens

12 September · On the Other Side of the Door · Jeff Moss

The American writer Jeff Moss was perhaps best known for his award-winning work on the children's television programme *Sesame Street*. He was also the writer of several collections of children's poetry.

On the other side of the door
I can be a different me,
As smart and as brave and as funny or strong
As a person could want to be.
There's nothing too hard for me to do,
There's no place I can't explore
Because everything can happen
On the other side of the door.

On the other side of the door
I don't have to go alone.
If you come, too, we can sail tall ships
And fly where the wind has flown.
And wherever we go, it is almost sure
We'll find what we're looking for
Because everything can happen
On the other side of the door.

☀ 13 September · Plums · Gillian Clarke

Across late summer and early autumn, plums are in
season. The Welsh poet Gillian Clarke traces plums
from the sweet ripeness of summer fruits to the skeletal
form of a plum-tree in winter.

When their time comes they fall
without wind, without rain.
They seep through the trees' muslin
in a slow fermentation.

Daily the low sun warms them
in a late love that is sweeter
than summer. In bed at night
we hear heartbeat of fruitfall.

The secretive slugs crawl home
to the burst honeys, are found
in the morning mouth on mouth,
inseparable.

We spread patchwork counterpanes
for a clean catch. Baskets fill,
never before such harvest,
such a hunters' moon burning

the hawthorns, drunk on syrups
that are richer by night
when spiders pitch
tents in the wet grass.

This morning the red sun
is opening like a rose
on our white wall, prints there
the fishbone shadow of a fern.

The early blackbirds fly
guilty from a dawn haul
of fallen fruit. We too
breakfast on sweetnesses.

Soon plum trees will be bone,
grown delicate with frost's
formalities. Their black
angles will tear the snow.

13 September • Now I Lay Me Down to Sleep • Anon.

This prayer-poem dates from the eighteenth century,
when Christian children were taught to pray at bedtime
for their safety and the safety of the ones they loved.

Now I lay me down to sleep,
I pray the Lord my soul to keep,
If I should die before I wake
I pray the Lord my soul to take.

14 September · *from* Annus Mirabilis · John Dryden

John Dryden was the very first Poet Laureate of Great Britain, and he is considered to be one of the finest poets of Restoration England, the period following Charles II's return to the throne in 1660. 'Annus Mirabilis' is a Latin phrase meaning 'wonderful year' or 'year of miracles', although the year Dryden writes of – 1666 – was marked by disasters throughout. The miracle, for Dryden, is that the world didn't end altogether, given that the date contained '666', the devilish 'number of the beast'. This extract recounts the tragedy of what became known as the Great Fire of London.

> Such was the Rise of this prodigious fire,
> Which, in mean Buildings first obscurely bred,
> From thence did soon to open Streets aspire,
> And straight to Palaces and Temples spread.
>
> The diligence of Trades and noiseful Gain,
> And luxury, more late, asleep were laid:
> All was the night's, and in her silent reign
> No sound the rest of Nature did invade.
>
> In this deep quiet, from what source unknown,
> Those seeds of Fire their fatal Birth disclose;
> And first, few scatt'ring Sparks about were blown,
> Big with the flames that to our Ruin rose.

Then in some close-pent Room it crept along,
And, smould'ring as it went, in silence fed;
Till th' infant Monster, with devouring strong,
Walk'd boldly upright with exalted head.

Now like some rich or mighty Murderer,
Too great for Prison, which he breaks with Gold,
Who fresher for new Mischiefs does appear
And dares the World to tax him with the old:

So 'scapes th' insulting Fire his narrow Jail,
And makes small outlets into open air:
There the fierce Winds his tender Force assail,
And beat him downward to his first repair.

The Winds, like crafty Courtesans, withheld
His Flames from burning, but to blow them more:
And every fresh attempt he is repell'd
With faint Denials, weaker than before.

And now no longer letted of his Prey,
He leaps up at it with enrag'd desire:
O'erlooks the Neighbours with a wide survey,
And nods at every House his threat'ning Fire.

'The Lord is my Shepherd' is among the most recognized of the poems contained in the Book of Psalms. Psalm 23 takes as its subject the relationship between God and man, comparing it to the relationship between a shepherd and his sheep. Psalms such as this one would have been treasured by the Puritan pilgrims who set sail for America around this date in September 1620: their journey across the Atlantic in search of a new life was a leap of faith, and the comfort of a deep trust in a loving God would have been indispensable.

The Lord is my shepherd; I shall not want.
He maketh me to lie down in green pastures: he leadeth me beside the still waters.
He restoreth my soul: he leadeth me in the paths of righteousness for his name's sake.
Yea, though I walk through the valley of the shadow of death, I will fear no evil: for thou art with me; thy rod and thy staff they comfort me.
Thou preparest a table before me in the presence of mine enemies: thou anointest my head with oil; my cup runneth over.
Surely goodness and mercy shall follow me all the days of my life: and I will dwell in the house of the Lord for ever.

15 September · The Mummy · Edwin Morgan

Edwin Morgan's poem imagines a conversation between the mummified body of Rameses II, an Egyptian pharaoh, and a modern specialist in the preservation of museum artefacts. Morgan's poem is comic, and draws freely on the literary legacy of Rameses, also known as Ozymandias (Percy Bysshe Shelley's poem, 'Ozymandias', alluded to by Morgan, appears in this book on 12 October). However, the events were also amusing in real life: to be flown to France, the mummy was issued an Egyptian passport that listed his occupation as 'King (deceased)'. The body was welcomed as a great head of state, and received by a military guard.

(The Mummy [of Rameses II] was met at Orly airport
by Mme Saunier-Seïté. – *News item, Sept. 1976*)

— May I welcome Your Majesty to Paris.

— Mm.

— I hope the flight from Cairo was reasonable.

— Mmmmm.

— We have a germ-proof room at the Museum of
   Man
where we trust Your Majesty will have peace and
   quiet.

— Unh-unh.

41

— I am sorry, but this is necessary.
You Majesty's person harbours a fungus.

— Fng fng's, hn?

— Well, it is something attacking your cells.
Your Majesty is gently deteriorating
after nearly four thousand years
becalmed in masterly embalmment.
We wish to save you from the worm.

— Wrm hrm! Mgh-mgh-mgh.

— Indeed I know it must be distressing
to a pharaoh and a son of Ra,
to the excavator of Abu Simbel
that glorious temple in the rock,
to the perfecter of Karnak hall,
to the hammer of the Hittites,
to the colossus whose colossus
raised in red granite at holy Thebes
sixteen-men-high astounds the desert
shattered, as Your Majesty in life
shattered the kingdom and oppressed the poor
with such lavish grandeur and panache,
to Ramses, to Ozymandias,
to the Louis Quatorze of the Nile,
how bitter it must be to feel
a microbe eat your camphored bands.
But we are here to help Your Majesty.
We shall encourage you to unwind.
You have many useful years ahead.

— M' n'm 'z 'zym'nidas, kng'v kngz!

— Yes yes. Well, Shelley is dead now.
He was not embalmed. He will not write
about Your Majesty again.

— T't'nkh'm'n? H'tsh'ps't?
'khn't'n? N'f'rt'ti? Mm? Mm?

— The hall of fame has many mansions.
Your Majesty may rest assured
your deeds will always be remembered.

— Youmm w'm'nn. B't'f'lll w'm'nnnn.
No w'm'nnn f'r th'zndz y'rz.

— Your Majesty, what are you doing?

— Ng! Mm. Mhm. Mm? Mm? Mmmmm.

— Your Majesty, Your Majesty! You'll break you
    stitches!

— Fng st'chez fng's wrm hrm.

— I really hate to have to use
a hypodermic on a mummy,
but we cannot have you strain yourself.
Remember your fungus, Your Majesty.

— Fng. Zzzzzzzz.

— That's right.

— Aaaaaaaaah.

According to The Bible, The Lord's Prayer is a prayer given by Jesus to his disciples during the Sermon on the Mount.

> Our Father, which art in heaven,
> Hallowed be thy Name.
> Thy Kingdom come.
> Thy will be done in earth,
> As it is in heaven.
> Give us this day our daily bread.
> And forgive us our trespasses,
> As we forgive them that trespass against us.
> And lead us not into temptation,
> But deliver us from evil.
> For thine is the kingdom,
> The power, and the glory,
> For ever and ever.
> Amen.

16 September · Old Ironsides · Oliver Wendell Holmes, Sr.

Oliver Wendell Holmes wrote this poem, about the eighteenth-century naval frigate USS *Constitution*, on 16 September 1830. She remains in Boston to this day, and is the oldest commissioned ship afloat in the world!

Ay, tear her tattered ensign down!
　　Long has it waved on high,
And many an eye has danced to see
　　That banner in the sky;
Beneath it rung the battle shout,
　　And burst the cannon's roar; –
The meteor of the ocean air
　　Shall sweep the clouds no more!

Her deck, once red with heroes' blood,
　　Where knelt the vanquished foe,
When winds were hurrying o'er the flood
　　And waves were white below,
No more shall feel the victor's tread,
　　Or know the conquered knee; –
The harpies of the shore shall pluck
　　The eagle of the sea!

45

O, better that her shattered hulk
   Should sink beneath the wave;
Her thunders shook the mighty deep,
   And there should be her grave;
Nail to the mast her holy flag,
   Set every thread-bare sail,
And give her to the god of storms,
   The lightning and the gale!

16 September · The Iroquois Prayer

This prayer of thanks is a tradition passed on by the Iroquois, a confederacy of Native American tribes who lived in upstate New York and the area surrounding the Great Lakes before the advent of the modern United States. There are still Iroquois communities living in Canada and America.

We return thanks to our mother, the earth, which sustains us.
We return thanks to the rivers and streams, which supply us with water.
We return thanks to all herbs, which furnish medicines for the cure of our diseases.
We return thanks to the corn, and to her sisters, the beans and squash, which give us life. We return thanks to the bushes and trees, which provide us with fruit.
We return thanks to the wind which, moving the air, has banished diseases.
We return thanks to the moon and the stars, which have given us their light when the sun was gone.
We return thanks to our grandfather He-no, who has given to us his rain.
We return thanks to the sun, that he has looked upon the earth with a beneficent eye. Lastly, we return thanks to the Great Spirit, in whom is embodied all goodness, and who directs all things for the good of his children.

17 September · Harriet Tubman · Eloise Greenfield

On this day in 1849, Harriet Tubman escaped from slavery in Maryland, before returning to rescue her family. Eventually her efforts led to the freeing of dozens of slaves. Later in life she fought for the Union Army in the American Civil War, and led a raid to free over 700 slaves from Southern plantations.

Harriet Tubman didn't take no stuff
Wasn't scared of nothing neither
Didn't come in this world to be no slave
And wasn't going to stay one either

'Farewell!' she sang to her friends one night
She was mighty sad to leave 'em
But she ran away that dark, hot night
Ran looking for her freedom
She ran to the woods and she ran through the woods
With the slave catchers right behind her
And she kept on going till she got to the North
Where those mean men couldn't find her

Nineteen times she went back South
To get three hundred others
She ran for her freedom nineteen times
To save Black sisters and brothers
Harriet Tubman didn't take no stuff
Wasn't scared of nothing neither
Didn't come in this world to be no slave
And didn't stay one either

And didn't stay one either

17 September · The Easterner's Prayer

This anonymous poem purports to be an English version of a Muslim prayer. It is not, however, a translation; references to the fact that the speaker is not actually an 'Easterner' both open and close the poem.

> I pray the prayer the Easterners do —
> May the peace of Allah abide with you!
> Wherever you stay, wherever you go,
> May the beautiful palms of Allah grow,
> Through days of labour and nights of rest,
> The love of good Allah make you blest,
> So I touch my heart as Easterners do —
> May the peace of Allah abide with you!
> Salaam Alaikum
> (Peace be unto you).

☀ 18 September · Joy · Hugo Williams

Autumn is the season for picking blackberries out of wild hedgerows. For many, the memory of picking berries is associated both with their sweet taste, but also with bramble scratches and nettle stings. Hugo Williams here reflects on joy as a kind of comfortable lack of extremes, where all experiences sit between being stung and relieving the sting.

Not so much a sting
as a faint burn

not so much a pain
as the memory of pain

the memory of tears
flowing freely down cheeks

in a sort of joy
that there was nothing

worse in the world
than stinging nettle stings

and nothing better
than cool dock leaves.

18 September · The Mool Mantar

Sikhism first developed in South Asia during the fifteenth century, and today there are over 25 million Sikhs living throughout the world. The Mool Mantar is the first line of the sacred book of the Sikhs, the Guru Granth Sahib; it outlines the basic beliefs of Sikhism regarding the nature of God as omnipresent and eternal.

Ik Onkar
There is only one God
Sat Nam
Eternal truth is His name
Karta Purakh
He is the creator
Nir Bhau
He is without fear
Nir Vair
He is without hate
Akal Murat
Immortal, without form
Ajuni
Beyond birth and death
Saibhang
He is the enlightener
Gur Prasaad
He can be reached through the mercy
    and grace of the true Guru

51

☀ 19 September · Now May Every Living Thing

With over 370 million followers worldwide, Buddhism is one of the world's major religions, and is centred on the teachings of Buddha, Siddhartha Gautama, who embarked on a quest for enlightenment around the sixth century BC. He is thought to have written the simple blessing printed here. While there are many different forms of Buddhism, and specific teachings vary accordingly, there are some important tenets which are shared between them all: a belief in pacifism and the importance of living a non-violent life; the notion that nothing is permanent or fixed, and that change is always possible; and an emphasis on the importance of meditation and self-development in order to reach a state of enlightenment, known as nirvana.

Now may every living thing, young or old, weak or strong, living near or far, known or unknown, living or departed or yet unborn, may every living thing be full of bliss.

19 September · Prologue · Patience Agbabi

Today begins a sequence of poems about words and language – the very stuff of poetry. Patience Agbabi grew up in London, the daughter of Nigerian parents. This poem is a veritable feast of wordplay and puns, all centring on the word 'word'.

Give me a word
any word
let it roll across your tongue
like a dolly mixture.
Open your lips
say it loud
let each syllable vibrate like a transistor
Say it again again again again again
till it's a tongue twister
till its meaning is in tatters
till its meaning equals sound
now write it down,
letter by letter
loop the loops
till you form a structure.
Do it again again again again again
till it's a word picture.
Does this inspire?
Is your consciousness on fire?
Then let me take you higher.

53

Give me a noun
give me a verb
and I'm in motion
cos I'm on a mission
to deliver information
so let me take you to the fifth dimension.
No fee, it's free,
you only gotta pay attention.
So sit back, relax,
let me take you back
to when you learnt to walk, talk,
learnt coordination
and communication,
mama
dada.
If you rub two words together you get friction
cut them in half, you get a fraction.
If you join two words you get multiplication.
My school of mathematics
equals verbal acrobatics
so let's make conversation.

Give me a preposition
give me an interjection
give me inspiration.
In the beginning was creation
I'm not scared of revelations
cos I've done my calculations.
I've got high hopes
on the tightrope,
I just keep talking.
I got more skills than i got melanin
I'm fired by adrenaline
if you wanna know what rhyme it is

it's feminine.
Cos I'm Eve on an Apple Mac
this is a rap attack
so rich in onomatopoeia
I'll take you higher than the ozone layer.
So give me Word for Windows
give me 'W' times three
cos I'm on a mission
to deliver information
that is gravity defying
and i'll keep on trying
till you lose your fear of flying.

Give me a pronoun
give me a verb
and I'm living in syntax.
You only need two words to form a sentence.
I am I am I am I am I am
bicultural and sometimes clinical
my mother fed me rhymes through the umbilical,
I was born waxing lyrical.
I was raised on Watch with Mother
The Rime of the Ancient Mariner
and Fight the Power.
Now I have the perfect tutor
in my postmodern suitor,
I'm in love with me computer.
But let me shut down
before I touch down.

Give me a word
give me a big word
let me manifest
express in excess
The M I X
of my voice box.
Now I've eaten the apple
I'm more subtle than a snake is.
I wanna do poetic things in poetic places
Give me poetry unplugged
so I can counter silence.
Give me my poetic licence

and I'll give you metaphors that top eclipses
I'll give you megabytes and megamixes.

Give me a stage and I'll cut form on it
give me a page and I'll perform on it.

Give me a word
any word.

20 September · Ars Poetica ·
Archibald MacLeish

What should a poem be? For Archibald MacLeish in this poem about silence and absence, it is enough that it should simply 'be'.

A poem should be palpable and mute
As a globed fruit,

Dumb
As old medallions to the thumb,

Silent as the sleeve-worn stone
Of casement ledges where the moss has grown –

A poem should be wordless
As the flight of birds.

*

A poem should be motionless in time
As the moon climbs,

Leaving, as the moon releases
Twig by twig the night-entangled trees,

Leaving, as the moon behind the winter leaves,
Memory by memory the mind –

A poem should be motionless in time
As the moon climbs.

*

A poem should be equal to:
Not true.

For all the history of grief
An empty doorway and a maple leaf.

For love
The leaning grasses and two lights above the sea —

A poem should not mean
But be.

20 September · Tichborne's Elegy · Chidiock Tichborne

On 20 September 1586, the poet Chidiock Tichborne was executed for his involvement in the conspiracy, known as the Babington Plot, to murder Queen Elizabeth I and replace her with the Catholic Mary Queen of Scots. On the eve of his execution, Tichborne wrote a letter to his wife Agnes in which he included this elegy.

My prime of youth is but a frost of cares;
My feast of joy is but a dish of pain,
My crop of corn is but a field of tares,
And all my good is but vain hope of gain:
The day is past, and yet I saw no sun,
And now I live, and now my life is done.

My tale was heard, and yet it was not told,
My fruit is fallen, and yet my leaves are green,
My youth is spent, and yet I am not old,
I saw the world, and yet I was not seen:
My thread is cut, and yet it is not spun,
And now I live, and now my life is done.

I sought my death, and found it in my womb,
I looked for life, and saw it was a shade,
I trod the earth, and knew it was my tomb,
And now I die, and now I was but made;
The glass is full, and now the glass is run,
And now I live, and now my life is done.

59

21 September • Shut Not Your Doors to Me, Proud Libraries • Walt Whitman

This poem was written by Whitman, one of the most celebrated of American poets, not long after the American Civil War and the assassination of President Lincoln in 1865. The book in this poem is a very strange one – its words are entirely unimportant and it seems to be alive! It is, perhaps, a metaphor for life itself and the knowledge we can receive just by living life joyfully.

Shut not your doors to me, proud libraries,
For that which was lacking among you all, yet needed
   most, I bring;
A book I have made for your dear sake, O soldiers,
And for you, O soul of man, and you, love of
   comrades;
The words of my book nothing, the life of it
   everything;
A book separate, not link'd with the rest, nor felt by
   the intellect;
But you will feel every word, O Libertad! arm'd
   Libertad!
It shall pass by the intellect to swim the sea, the air,
With joy with you, O soul of man.

21 September · Pied Beauty ·
Gerard Manley Hopkins

In this poem, Gerard Manley Hopkins uses 'dappled things' to mean those that are not traditionally considered beautiful, defending diversity and variety.

Glory be to God for dappled things –
  For skies of couple-colour as a brinded cow;
    For rose-moles all in stipple upon trout that swim;
Fresh-firecoal chestnut-falls; finches' wings;
  Landscape plotted and pieced – fold, fallow, and plough;
    And áll trádes, their gear and tackle and trim.

All things counter, original, spare, strange;
  Whatever is fickle, freckled (who knows how?)
    With swift, slow; sweet, sour; adazzle, dim;
He fathers-forth whose beauty is past change:
                    Praise him.

22 September · An Old Woman of the Roads · Padraic Colum

Padraic Colum was a celebrated Irish poet and playwright of the twentieth century. He corresponded with many great poets, including W. B. Yeats, and was a lifelong friend of the novelist James Joyce. This poem, told from the point of view of a homeless woman, asks us to appreciate the material things we take for granted – a clock, a hearth, and, above all, a roof above our heads.

O, to have a little house!
To own the hearth and stool and all!
The heaped up sods upon the fire,
The pile of turf against the wall!

To have a clock with weights and chains
And pendulum swinging up and down!
A dresser filled with shining delph,
Speckled and white and blue and brown!

I could be busy all the day
Clearing and sweeping hearth and floor,
And fixing on their shelf again
My white and blue and speckled store!

I could be quiet there at night
Beside the fire and by myself,
Sure of a bed and loth to leave
The ticking clock and the shining delph!

Och! but I'm weary of mist and dark,
And roads where there's never a house nor bush,
And tired I am of bog and road,
And the crying wind and the lonesome hush!

And I am praying to God on high,
And I am praying Him night and day,
For a little house – a house of my own –
Out of the wind's and the rain's way.

22 September · *from* Meditation XVII · John Donne

On 22 September 1735, Robert Walpole, who is considered the first Prime Minister of Great Britain, took up residence in 10 Downing Street — a town house in central London which, to this day, is the official home of the British Prime Minister. Edward Heath, who was the British Prime Minster from 1970–1974, quoted these famous (prose) lines by John Donne and added, 'Today no island is an island. That applies as much to the price of bread as it does to political influence.'

No man is an island entire of itself; every man is a piece of the continent, a part of the main; if a clod be washed away by the sea, Europe is the less, as well as if a promontory were, as well as any manner of thy friends or of thine own were; any man's death diminishes me, because I am involved in mankind. And therefore never send to know for whom the bell tolls; it tolls for thee.

23 September · Digging · Edward Thomas

Around this date is the autumn equinox, where, due to the tilt of the earth in relation to the sun, the length of night and day is almost exactly the same across the entire globe. The literal meaning of 'equinox' is 'equal night'. Edward Thomas's autumn poem is not about light and sight, though, but about the smells that we associate with this season.

Today I think
Only with scents, – scents dead leaves yield,
And bracken, and wild carrot's seed,
And the square mustard field;

Odours that rise
When the spade wounds the roots of tree,
Rose, currant, raspberry, or goutweed,
Rhubarb or celery;

The smoke's smell, too,
Flowing from where a bonfire burns
The dead, the waste, the dangerous,
And all to sweetness turns.

It is enough
To smell, to crumble the dark earth,
While the robin sings over again
Sad songs of Autumn mirth.

☾ **23 September** · When I Heard the Learn'd Astronomer · Walt Whitman

On this day in 1846, the German astronomer Johann Gottfried Galle discovered the planet Neptune. An 'astronomer' is a scientist who studies stars, planets and space. Walt Whitman wrote this poem in 1865, so the astronomer in this poem might have mentioned Neptune in his lecture.

When I heard the learn'd astronomer,
When the proofs, the figures, were ranged in columns
    before me,
When I was shown the charts and diagrams, to add,
    divide, and measure them,
When I sitting heard the astronomer where he lectured
    with much applause in the lecture-room,
How soon unaccountable I became tired and sick,
Till rising and gliding out I wander'd off by myself,
In the mystical moist night-air, and from time to time,
Look'd up in perfect silence at the stars.

24 September · Autumn Fires ·
Robert Louis Stevenson

Autumn brings with it cold weather and the coming
of darker nights, as we transition from the warmth
of summer to the chill of winter. However, in this
delightful poem, Stevenson finds 'something bright' in
every season, as he celebrates the tradition of bonfires.

> In the other gardens
>   And all up the vale,
> From the autumn bonfires
>   See the smoke trail!
>
> Pleasant summer over
>   And all the summer flowers,
> The red fire blazes,
>   The grey smoke towers.
>
> Sing a song of seasons!
>   Something bright in all!
> Flowers in the summer,
>   Fires in the fall!

☾ 24 September · A Psalm of Life ·
Henry Wadsworth Longfellow

On this day in 1940, King George VI instituted the George Cross – a silver cross-shaped medal that could be awarded for acts of heroism outside the battlefield. This inspirational poem by the American writer Henry Wadsworth Longfellow encourages its audience to be positive and heroic in life, in 'the world's broad field of battle'.

What the Heart of the Young Man
Said to the Psalmist.

Tell me not, in mournful numbers,
   'Life is but an empty dream!'
For the soul is dead that slumbers,
   And things are not what they seem.

Life is real! Life is earnest!
   And the grave is not its goal;
'Dust thou art, to dust returnest,'
   Was not spoken of the soul.

Not enjoyment, and not sorrow,
   Is our destined end or way;
But to act, that each to-morrow
   Find us farther than to-day.

Art is long, and Time is fleeting,
  And our hearts, though stout and brave,
Still, like muffled drums, are beating
  Funeral marches to the grave.

In the world's broad field of battle,
  In the bivouac of Life,
Be not like dumb, driven cattle!
  Be a hero in the strife!

Trust no Future, howe'er pleasant!
  Let the dead Past bury its dead!
Act,— act in the living Present!
  Heart within, and God o'erhead!

Lives of great men all remind us
  We can make our lives sublime,
And, departing, leave behind us
  Footprints on the sands of time;

Footprints, that perhaps another,
  Sailing o'er life's solemn main,
A forlorn and shipwrecked brother,
  Seeing, shall take heart again.

Let us, then, be up and doing,
  With a heart for any fate;
Still achieving, still pursuing,
  Learn to labour and to wait.

25 September · Something Told the Wild Geese · Rachel Field

At this time of year, many kinds of birds will migrate south, travelling from their breeding grounds in the north to a warm place for winter. Geese fly in a V-formation in order to reduce air resistance and help them conserve energy for their long flights, which can be many thousands of miles. Rachel Field's poem observes the way in which birds, seemingly mysteriously, know when the seasons are turning, and when they must migrate.

Something told the wild geese
  It was time to go.
Though the fields lay golden
  Something whispered, – 'Snow.'

Leaves were green and stirring,
  Berries, lustre-glossed,
But beneath warm feathers
  Something cautioned, – 'Frost.'

All the sagging orchards
  Steamed with amber spice,
But each wild breast stiffened
  At remembered Ice.

Something told the wild geese
  It was time to fly, –
Summer sun was on their wings,
  Winter in their cry.

25 September · Wild Geese · Mary Oliver

In this poem, the Pulitzer Prize-winning poet Mary Oliver uses the image of wild geese flying home as a metaphor for the way in which the world impacts on us – sounds and sights are like birds, flying home to us.

You do not have to be good.
You do not have to walk on your knees
for a hundred miles through the desert, repenting.
You only have to let the soft animal of your body
love what it loves.
Tell me about your despair, yours, and I will tell you mine.
Meanwhile the world goes on.
Meanwhile the sun and the clear pebbles of the rain
are moving across the landscapes,
over the prairies and the deep trees,
the mountains and the rivers.
Meanwhile the wild geese, high in the clean blue air,
are heading home again.
Whoever you are, no matter how lonely,
the world offers itself to your imagination,
calls to you like the wild geese, harsh and exciting –
over and over announcing your place
in the family of things.

26 September · Astrophysics Lesson · Ade Hall

Have you ever looked up at the sky and wondered how it all works? How is the moon held in place, and why does it sometimes disappear? Why does the sun set, and how far away are those stars? In this poem a school teacher uses fruit to try to demonstrate the positions of stars and planets.

I took an orange and a plum
To demonstrate the Earth and Sun;
held in place by gravity –
Our little planet, you and me.

I grabbed some grapes for all the stars
And cast them out so wide and far;
Distant suns and foreign moons
In all four corners of the room.

The wonders of the galaxy
Spread out before class 2BT.
'Where did they come from?' someone cried;
'From the fruit bowl' I replied.

26 September · The Tyger · William Blake

'The Tyger' is taken from William Blake's 1794 collection *Songs of Experience*, and is one of his most memorable poems. Blake's tiger is certainly terrifying, stalking 'the forests of the night' with its burning eyes.

Tyger, Tyger, burning bright,
In the forests of the night;
What immortal hand or eye
Could frame thy fearful symmetry?

In what distant deeps or skies.
Burnt the fire of thine eyes?
On what wings dare he aspire?
What the hand, dare seize the fire?

And what shoulder, & what art,
Could twist the sinews of thy heart?
And when thy heart began to beat,
What dread hand? & what dread feet?

What the hammer? what the chain?
In what furnace was thy brain?
What the anvil? what dread grasp,
Dare its deadly terrors clasp?

When the stars threw down their spears
And water'd heaven with their tears:
Did he smile his work to see?
Did he who made the Lamb make thee?

73

Tyger, Tyger, burning bright,
In the forests of the night:
What immortal hand or eye
Dare frame thy fearful symmetry?

27 September · The Railway Children · Seamus Heaney

On this day in 1825, the engineer George Stephenson's steam engine *Locomotion* was taken out on the railways for the first time. It was the first passenger journey ever made by rail. Seamus Heaney, who died in 2013, was a great Irish poet, and the winner of the Nobel Prize for Literature in 1995. The title of this poem references Edith Nesbit's 1905 novel *The Railway Children*. It plays with the difference between knowledge and imagination: the children do not know how telegraphs work, but the narrator is enrapt as he thinks of words streaming down the wires.

When we climbed the slopes of the cutting
We were eye-level with the white cups
Of the telegraph poles and the sizzling wires.

Like lovely freehand they curved for miles
East and miles west beyond us, sagging
Under their burden of swallows.

We were small and thought we knew nothing
Worth knowing. We thought words travelled the wires
In the shiny pouches of raindrops,

Each one seeded full with the light
Of the sky, the gleam of the lines, and ourselves
So infinitesimally scaled

We could stream through the eye of a needle.

☾ **27 September** • My Boy Jack •
Rudyard Kipling

John Kipling, who was known as Jack, was the only son of the poet Rudyard Kipling. When the First World War broke out in 1914, his father used his influence to get Jack a military commission, despite his poor eyesight. Jack went missing in the Battle of Loos on the 27 September 1915, six weeks after his eighteenth birthday. His body was not found in the aftermath of the battle, and it was not until 1992 that his grave was identified in St Mary's Cemetery, Haisnes.

'Have you news of my boy Jack?'
    Not this tide.
'When d'you think that he'll come back?'
    Not with this wind blowing, and this tide.

'Has any one else had word of him?'
    Not this tide.
For what is sunk will hardly swim,
    Not with this wind blowing, and this tide.

'Oh, dear, what comfort can I find?'
    None this tide,
    Nor any tide,
Except he did not shame his kind—
    Not even with that wind blowing, and that tide.

Then hold your head up all the more,
    This tide,
    And every tide;
Because he was the son you bore,
    And gave to that wind blowing and that tide!

28 September ✳ Barrier ✳ Rachel Rooney

Rachel Rooney composed this poem for the theme of National Poetry Day 2017, which was 'freedom'. This works as a visual reminder of the power of words to overcome barriers.

BARRIERBARRIERBARRIER
BARRIERBARRIERBARRIER
BARRIERBARRIERBARRIER
BARRIERFREEDOM**BARRIER**
BARRIERBARRIERBARRIER
BARRIERBARRIERBARRIER
BARRIERBARRIERBARRIER

BARRIERBARRIERBARRIER
BARRIERBARRIERBARRIER
BARRIERBARRIERBARRIER
BARRIER   *FREEDOM***BARRIER**
BARRIERBARRIERBARRIER
BARRIERBARRIERBARRIER
BARRIERBARRIERBARRIER

BARRIERBARRIERBARRIER
BARRIERBARRIERBARRIER
BARRIERBARRIERBARRIER
BARRIER   BARRIER   **FREEDOM**
BARRIERBARRIERBARRIER
BARRIERBARRIERBARRIER
BARRIERBARRIERBARRIER

77

🌙 28 September · Full Moon and Little Frieda · Ted Hughes

Ted Hughes wrote this poem in 1962, when he was living in Devon. It describes an incident that happened in the garden of his house, Court Green, with his young daughter Frieda.

A cool small evening shrunk to a dog bark and the
    clank of a bucket –

And you listening.
A spider's web, tense for the dew's touch.
A pail lifted, still and brimming – mirror
To tempt a first star to a tremor.

Cows are going home in the lane there, looping the
    hedges with their warm wreaths of breath –
A dark river of blood, many boulders,
Balancing unspilled milk.

'Moon!' you cry suddenly, 'Moon! Moon!'

The moon has stepped back like an artist gazing
    amazed at a work

That points at him amazed.

29 September • Autumn Rain • D. H. Lawrence

In this poem, D. H. Lawrence is at once speaking of
the bitterness of autumn weather and the tragedy of
warfare. The poem surprises us by introducing fallen
men, but locks the two sets of images, of weather and
war, together through its extraordinarily tight pattern of
rhymes, which echo across the poem.

The plane leaves
fall black and wet
on the lawn;

the cloud sheaves
in heaven's fields set
droop and are drawn

in falling seeds of rain;
the seed of heaven
on my face

falling – I hear again
like echoes even
that softly pace

heaven's muffled floor,
the winds that tread
out all the grain

79

of tears, the store
harvested
in the sheaves of pain

caught up aloft:
the sheaves of dead
men that are slain

now winnowed soft
on the floor of heaven;
manna invisible

of all the pain
here to us given;
finely divisible
falling as rain.

29 September · The Song of Mr Toad · Kenneth Grahame

Kenneth Grahame is best known for writing *The Wind in the Willows*, a much-loved children's classic documenting the adventures of four characterful animals: Rat, Mole, Badger and the subject of this poem, the charismatic but bonkers Mr Toad.

The world has held great Heroes,
As history-books have showed;
But never a name to go down to fame
Compared with that of Toad!

The clever men at Oxford
Know all that there is to be knowed.
But they none of them knew one half as much
As intelligent Mr Toad!

The animals sat in the Ark and cried,
Their tears in torrents flowed.
Who was it said, 'There's land ahead'?
Encouraging Mr Toad!

The Army all saluted
As they marched along the road.
Was it the King? Or Kitchener?
No. It was Mr Toad!

The Queen and her Ladies-in-waiting
Sat at the window and sewed.
She cried, 'Look! who's that handsome man?'
They answered, 'Mr Toad.'

30 September · Thirty Days Hath September · Anon.

This is a traditional 'mnemonic' – a poem used to remember facts, in this case the number of days in each month. It's perhaps most often recited without the last two lines, but versions of the full six-line poem have been around since the sixteenth century.

Thirty days hath September,
April, June, and November;
All the rest have thirty-one,
Except for February alone,
And that has twenty-eight days clear
And twenty-nine in each leap year.

30 September · Thirty Days Hath September · Michael Rosen

This rhyming couplet lampoons the famous rhyme for remembering how many days there are in each month. The speaker of this poem only manages one month out of twelve – luckily his ability to find rhymes is much stronger than his memory!

> Thirty days hath September,
> All the rest I can't remember.

October

1 October · The Road Not Taken · Robert Frost

This is among the most popular of Frost's poems today, and its central image, of the road 'less traveled by' has entered into common language as an alternative phrase to 'off the beaten path'. The poem is a reflection on the necessity of choosing.

Two roads diverged in a yellow wood,
And sorry I could not travel both
And be one traveler, long I stood
And looked down one as far as I could
To where it bent in the undergrowth;

Then took the other, as just as fair,
And having perhaps the better claim,
Because it was grassy and wanted wear;
Though as for that the passing there
Had worn them really about the same,

And both that morning equally lay
In leaves no step had trodden black.
Oh, I kept the first for another day!
Yet knowing how way leads on to way,
I doubted if I should ever come back.

I shall be telling this with a sigh
Somewhere ages and ages hence:
Two roads diverged in a wood, and I –
I took the one less traveled by,
And that has made all the difference.

☾ 1 October · Messages · Matt Goodfellow

National Poetry Day in the UK usually falls on the first
Thursday in October. This poem was especially written
for National Poetry Day 2016's theme: 'messages'.

look closely and you'll find them
everywhere

in fields of patterned grasses
drafted by the hare

embroidered by the bluebells
through a wood

in scattered trails of blossom
stamped into the mud

scorched by heather-fire
across the moors

in looping snail-trails
scrawled on forest floors

scored across the sky
by screaming swifts

in rolling, twisting peaks
of drifting mountain mist

scribbled by an ocean
on the sand

look closely: you will see
and understand

2 October · Fall, Leaves, Fall · Emily Brontë

Emily Brontë was a poet and novelist who lived in the West Riding of Yorkshire, England. She is best known for her novel, *Wuthering Heights*, which was published in 1847.

> Fall, leaves, fall; die, flowers, away;
> Lengthen night and shorten day;
> Every leaf speaks bliss to me
> Fluttering from the autumn tree.
> I shall smile when wreaths of snow
> Blossom where the rose should grow;
> I shall sing when night's decay
> Ushers in a drearier day.

☾ 2 October · Moonlit Apples · John Drinkwater

Autumn is the season for apples. The poet and
playwright John Drinkwater offers this poem about
freshly picked apples, with an allusion to Robert Burns's
'To a Mouse' and his 'best laid plans of mice and men'.

At the top of the house the apples are laid in rows,
And the skylight lets the moonlight in, and those
Apples are deep-sea apples of green. There goes
    A cloud on the moon in the autumn night.

A mouse in the wainscot scratches, and scratches, and
    then
There is no sound at the top of the house of men
Or mice; and the cloud is blown, and the moon again
    Dapples the apples with deep-sea light.

They are lying in rows there, under the gloomy beams;
On the sagging floor; they gather the silver streams
Out of the moon, those moonlit apples of dreams,
    And quiet is the steep stair under.

In the corridors under there is nothing but sleep.
And stiller than ever on orchard boughs they keep
Tryst with the moon, and deep is the silence, deep
    On moon-washed apples of wonder.

3 October · Crab-Apples · Imtiaz Dharker

Have you ever smelt or eaten a particular food and found yourself suddenly thinking of people or places you'd entirely forgotten? Imtiaz Dharker, who was born in Lahore, Pakistan, and whose parents were both Pakistani, plays with ideas of place, home, and identity, as local ingredients are turned into nostalgic reminders of the past.

> My mother picked crab-apples
> off the Glasgow apple trees
> and pounded them with chillies
> to change
> her homesickness
> into green chutney.

☾ 3 October · Pencil and Paint · Eleanor Farjeon

In the two verses of this poem, Eleanor Farjeon uses drawing and painting to compare the visual differences between Autumn and Winter.

Winter has a pencil
For pictures clear and neat,
She traces the black tree-tops
Upon a snowy sheet.

But autumn has a palette
And a painting-brush instead,
And daubs the leaves for pleasure
With yellow, brown, and red.

4 October · Santa Filomena ·
Henry Wadsworth Longfellow

In October 1853 the Crimean War broke out, lasting until March 1856. It was fought between Russia on one side, and an alliance of Britain, France, the Ottoman Empire, and the Kingdom of Sardinia on the other. The war became notorious for tactical and medical blunders by all parties. 'The Lady of the Lamp' Florence Nightingale rose to prominence during the Crimean War through her use of groundbreaking nursing methods on the wounded, and through her activism of progressive and professional medical care. Nightingale features in this poem by Longfellow.

Whene'er a noble deed is wrought,
Whene'er is spoken a noble thought,
        Our hearts, in glad surprise,
        To higher levels rise.

The tidal wave of deeper souls
Into our inmost being rolls,
        And lifts us unawares
        Out of all meaner cares.

Honor to those whose words or deeds
Thus help us in our daily needs,
        And by their overflow
        Raise us from what is low!

Thus thought I, as by night I read
Of the great army of the dead,
        The trenches cold and damp,
        The starved and frozen camp, –

The wounded from the battle-plain,
In dreary hospitals of pain,
    The cheerless corridors,
    The cold and stony floors.

Lo! in that house of misery
A lady with a lamp I see
    Pass through the glimmering gloom,
    And flit from room to room.

And slow, as in a dream of bliss,
The speechless sufferer turns to kiss
    Her shadow, as it falls
    Upon the darkening walls.

As if a door in heaven should be
Opened, and then closed suddenly,
    The vision came and went,
    The light shone was spent.

On England's annals, through the long
Hereafter of her speech and song,
    That light its rays shall cast
    From portals of the past.

A Lady with a Lamp shall stand
In the great history of the land,
    A noble type of good,
    Heroic womanhood.

Nor even shall be wanting here
The palm, the lily, and the spear,
    The symbols that of yore
    Saint Filomena bore.

4 October · St Francis and the Birds · Seamus Heaney

St Francis of Assisi was the founder of the Franciscan order of the Catholic Church, and he is remembered and celebrated for his special relationship with animals, which is what Seamus Heaney is drawing on in this poem. He is also known for his generosity to the poor and his willingness to help lepers. He died on 4 October 1226, and he was canonized as a saint in 1228.

When Francis preached love to the birds
They listened, fluttered, throttled up
Into the blue like a flock of words
Released for fun from his holy lips.
Then wheeled back, whirred about his head,
Pirouetted on brothers' capes.
Danced on the wing, for sheer joy played
And sang, like images took flight.
Which was the best poem Francis made,
His argument true, his tone light.

93

Abou Ben Adhem was a Muslim mystic – also known as a Sufi – who lived in Persia, and was venerated as a saint after his death, which happened around AD 777. He is often compared to St Francis of Assisi, because he gave up a luxurious life in favour of one devoted to prayer and helping his fellow man.

Abou Ben Adhem (may his tribe increase!)
Awoke one night from a deep dream of peace,
And saw, within the moonlight in his room,
Making it rich, and like a lily in bloom,
An angel writing in a book of gold:—
Exceeding peace had made Ben Adhem bold,
And to the presence in the room he said,
'What writest thou?'—The vision raised its head,
And with a look made of all sweet accord,
Answered, 'The names of those who love the Lord.'
'And is mine one?' said Abou. 'Nay, not so,'
Replied the angel. Abou spoke more low,
But cheerly still; and said, 'I pray thee, then,
Write me as one that loves his fellow men.'

The angel wrote, and vanished. The next night
It came again with a great wakening light,
And showed the names whom love of God had blest,
And lo! Ben Adhem's name led all the rest.

5 October · Autumn · T. E. Hulme

Hulme's poem on autumn stands out as an exemplar of the modernist movement in poetry: written in free-verse, without rhyme, and leaving the reader to make sense of its images. What kind of meaningful exchange can occur between the solitary walker and the bright night sky?

> A touch of cold in the Autumn night —
> I walked abroad,
> And saw the ruddy moon lean over a hedge
> Like a red-faced farmer.
> I did not stop to speak, but nodded,
> And round about were the wistful stars
> With white faces like town children.

6 October · *from* The Tyndale Bible

The death by execution of William Tyndale took place in October 1536, and is commemorated on this day. A scholar and skilled writer, he was most notable for his translation of the Bible into English, the best part of a century before the King James Version which is based on his translation. Translations of the Bible into English at the time were strictly prohibited, and Tyndale was forced to flee; he lived for a while in Antwerp before he was tracked down by Henry VIII's men and brought back to England. He was charged with heresy and burnt at the stake – all for trying to make the Bible more accessible. His final words were said to be: 'Lord, open the king of England's eyes.' These lines come from his translation of the Book of Exodus and speak of the oppression of the Israelites.

And Moses and Aaron came in vnto Pharaoh, and saide vnto him, Thus saith the Lord God of the Hebrewes, How long wilt thou refuse to humble thy selfe before mee? let my people goe, that they may serue me.

6 October · The Pheasant · Sylvia Plath

In this poem, the American poet Sylvia Plath is
addressing her husband, Ted Hughes. Hughes was a
keen game-shooter, having grown up in the Yorkshire
countryside, and Plath is asking him not to kill the
pheasant of the poem's title.

You said you would kill it this morning.
Do not kill it. It startles me still,
The jut of that odd, dark head, pacing

Through the uncut grass on the elm's hill.
It is something to own a pheasant,
Or just to be visited at all.

I am not mystical: it isn't
As if I thought it had a spirit.
It is simply in its element.

That gives it a kingliness, a right.
The print of its big foot last winter,
The trail-track, on the snow in our court

The wonder of it, in that pallor,
Through crosshatch of sparrow and starling.
Is it its rareness, then? It is rare.

But a dozen would be worth having,
A hundred, on that hill – green and red,
Crossing and recrossing: a fine thing!

It is such a good shape, so vivid.
It's a little cornucopia.
It unclaps, brown as a leaf, and loud,

Settles in the elm, and is easy.
It was sunning in the narcissi.
I trespass stupidly. Let be, let be.

7 October · *from* 1777 · Amy Lowell

This poem refers to the Battle of Saratoga which was fought on 7 October 1777, and marked a turning point in the American Revolutionary War, leading to America's freedom from the British Empire.

I – THE TRUMPET-VINE ARBOR

The throats of the little red trumpet-flowers are wide open,
And the clangor of brass beats against the hot sunlight.
They bray and blare at the burning sky.
Red! Red! Coarse notes of red,
Trumpeted at the blue sky.
In long streaks of sound, molten metal,
The vine declares itself.
Clang! – from its red and yellow trumpets;
Clang! – from its long, nasal trumpets,
Splitting the sunlight into ribbons, tattered and shot
     with noise.
I sit in the cool arbor, in a green and gold twilight.
It is very still, for I cannot hear the trumpets,
I only know that they are red and open,
And that the sun above the arbor shakes with heat.
My quill is newly mended,
And makes fine-drawn lines with its point.
Down the long white paper it makes little lines,
Just lines – up – down – criss-cross.
My heart is strained out at the pin-point of my quill;
It is thin and writhing like the marks of the pen.
My hand marches to a squeaky tune,
It marches down the paper to a squealing of fifes.

My pen and the trumpet-flowers,
And Washington's armies away over the smoke-tree to
  the southwest.
'Yankee Doodle,' my darling! It is you against the British,
Marching in your ragged shoes to batter down King
  George.
What have you got in your hat? Not a feather, I wager.
Just a hay-straw, for it is the harvest you are fighting for.
Hay in your hat, and the whites of their eyes for a target!
Like Bunker Hill, two years ago, when I watched all day
  from the housetop,
Through Father's spy-glass,
The red city, and the blue, bright water,
And puffs of smoke which you made.
Twenty miles away,
Round by Cambridge, or over the Neck,
But the smoke was white – white!
To-day the trumpet flowers are red – red –
And I cannot see you fighting;
But old Mr. Dimond has fled to Canada,
And Myra sings 'Yankee Doodle' at her milking.

The red throats of the trumpets bray and clang in the
  sunshine,
And the smoke-tree puffs dun blossoms into the blue air.

7 October · Birthday · Rachel Rooney

Autumn is a time when the wind starts blowing strongly, pulling leaves off trees and turning umbrellas inside out. In this poem Rachel Rooney personifies the wind, transforming it into a character having a tantrum on their birthday.

Wind was angry,
slammed the door.
Smash went the glass
on the kitchen floor.

Out in the garden
Wind shook trees,
kicked up a fuss
and a pile of leaves.

Wind was howling,
started to shout.
Who blew the candles
on my birthday cake out?

8 October · Lord Ullin's Daughter · Thomas Campbell

This ballad by Thomas Campbell, set in the Scottish highlands, tells the tale of a dangerous journey through a storm. While the autumnal wind in the Rooney poem knocks over glasses and slams doors, in 'Lord Ullin's Daughter' the storm impacts the lives of those who travel in it in a far more tragic way.

A Chieftain, to the Highlands bound,
　　Cries, 'Boatman, do not tarry;
And I'll give thee a silver pound
　　To row us o'er the ferry.'

'Now who be ye would cross Lochgyle,
　　This dark and stormy water?'
'Oh! I'm the chief of Ulva's isle,
　　And this Lord Ullin's daughter.

'And fast before her father's men
　　Three days we've fled together,
For should he find us in the glen,
　　My blood would stain the heather.

'His horsemen hard behind us ride;
　　Should they our steps discover,
Then who will cheer my bonny bride
　　When they have slain her lover?'

Outspoke the hardy Highland wight:
　'I'll go, my chief – I'm ready:
It is not for your silver bright,
　But for your winsome lady.

'And by my word, the bonny bird
　In danger shall not tarry:
So, though the waves are raging white,
　I'll row you o'er the ferry.'

By this the storm grew loud apace,
　The water-wraith was shrieking;
And in the scowl of heaven each face
　Grew dark as they were speaking.

But still, as wilder blew the wind,
　And as the night grew drearer,
Adown the glen rode armed men –
　Their trampling sounded nearer.

'Oh! Haste thee, haste!' the lady cries,
　'Though tempests round us gather;
I'll meet the raging of the skies,
　But not an angry father.'

The boat has left a stormy land,
　A stormy sea before her –
When oh! Too strong for human hand,
　The tempest gathered o'er her.

And still they rowed amidst the roar
　Of waters fast prevailing;
Lord Ullin reach'd that fatal shore –
　His wrath was chang'd to wailing.

For sore dismay'd, through storm and shade,
   His child he did discover;
One lovely hand she stretch'd for aid,
   And one was round her lover.

'Come back! Come back!' he cried in grief,
   'Across this stormy water;
And I'll forgive your Highland chief,
   My daughter! – oh, my daughter!'

'Twas vain: the loud waves lash'd the shore,
   Return or aid preventing;
The waters wild went o'er his child,
   And he was left lamenting.

8 October • Thumbprint • Eve Merriam

No two thumbprints are the same, and here the poet expands this thought to celebrate the fact that we are all unique and have our own individual role to play in history.

On the pad of my thumb
are whorls, whirls, wheels
in a unique design:
mine alone.
What a treasure to own!
My own flesh, my own feelings.
No other, however grand or base,
can ever contain the same.
My signature,
thumbing the pages of my time.
My universe key,
my singularity.
Impress, implant,
I am myself,
of all my atom parts I am the sum.
And out of my blood and my brain
I make my own interior weather,
my own sun and rain.
Imprint my mark upon the world
whatever I shall become.

☀ 9 October · Malala · Michaela Morgan

On 9 October, 2012, the Pakistani writer and activist Malala Yousafzai was shot by a Taliban gunman. At the time she was only fifteen. Though she was seriously injured, she lived, and her story was thrown into the centre of media attention. She went on to put her energies into working for the right of all children to an education, and at the age of seventeen she became the youngest ever recipient of a Nobel Peace Prize.

A girl with a book.
A girl with a book.
That's what has scared them –
A girl, with a book.

They get on to the bus.
They call out my name.
They aim. And they fire.
A shot to the brain.

Because a girl with a book,
A girl with a voice,
A girl with a brain,
A girl with a choice,
A girl with a plan
To have rights, like a man.
That's what they're scared of
One girl, with a book.

A girl who has words.
A girl with a pen.
A girl to be heard
With support of her friends
Who want to live free –
That' s what they fear,
A girl just like me.

9 October · She Dwelt Among the Untrodden Ways · William Wordsworth

This short lyric is one of Wordsworth's series of five poems that focused upon unrequited love for the eponymous Lucy, who may or may not have actually existed.

She dwelt among the untrodden ways
    Beside the springs of Dove,
A Maid whom there were none to praise
    And very few to love:

A violet by a mossy stone
    Half hidden from the eye!
— Fair as a star, when only one
    Is shining in the sky.

She lived unknown, and few could know
    When Lucy ceased to be;
But she is in her grave, and, oh,
    The difference to me!

10 October · Give · Simon Armitage

10 October is World Homeless Day, an international day of awareness for the global problem of homelessness and extreme poverty. Simon Armitage, who was appointed the UK Poet Laureate in May 2019, addresses in this poem the idea that other people's homelessness can seem like an inconvenience to us. But it is far worse, he tells us, to be the one without a home.

Of all the public places, dear,
to make a scene, I've chosen here.

Of all the doorways in the world
to choose to sleep, I've chosen yours.
I'm on the street, under the stars.

For coppers I can dance or sing.
For silver – swallow swords, eat fire.
For gold – escape from locks and chains.

It's not as if I'm holding out
for frankincense or myrrh, just change.

You give me tea. That's big of you.
I'm on my knees. I beg of you.

🌙 10 October · Xbox, Xbox – A Love Poem · Kenn Nesbitt

Ada Lovelace was a talented British mathematician, and daughter of poet Lord Byron. She is widely considered to be the first computer programmer due to her significant work in the 1830s on her friend Babbage's Analytical Engine. Ada Lovelace Day, the annual commemoration of her and her achievements, falls in October, and also celebrates the ongoing achievements of women in Science, Technology, Mathematics and Engineering.

Xbox, Xbox,
you're the one for me.
I also love my 3DS
and my Nintendo Wii.

GameCube, GameBoy,
Apple iPod Touch.
I never thought that I would ever
be in love this much.

Pac-Man, Sonic,
Mario, and Link.
Your names are etched inside my mind
in everlasting ink.

Run, jump, flip, hang,
double-jump, and climb.
That's all I want to do
with every second of my time.

This is true love.
Yes, it's plain to see.
Xbox, Xbox,
will you marry me?

11 October · Drummer Hodge · Thomas Hardy

The Boer War, fought between the British and the Boer States of South Africa, began on this day in 1899. It would last for three years. In this poem, Hardy uses South African words for the landscape – 'kopje', a rocky outcrop; 'veldt', grasslands; 'karoo', semi-desert – to create a sense of unfamiliarity. And yet, because of the tragedy of war, Drummer Hodge himself is now a part of that 'unknown plain'.

They throw in Drummer Hodge, to rest
　　Uncoffined – just as found:
His landmark is a kopje-crest
　　That breaks the veldt around;
And foreign constellations west
　　Each night above his mound.

Young Hodge the drummer never knew –
　　Fresh from his Wessex home –
The meaning of the broad Karoo,
　　The Bush, the dusty loam,
And why uprose to nightly view
　　Strange stars amid the gloom.

Yet portion of that unknown plain
　　Will Hodge for ever be;
His homely Northern breast and brain
　　Grow to some Southern tree,
And strange-eyed constellations reign
　　His stars eternally.

11 October · Kubla Khan · Samuel Taylor Coleridge

Written in October 1797 but not published until 1816, Samuel Taylor Coleridge claimed that 'Kubla Khan' was inspired by a dream. In a preface to his 1816 collection, he describes how he woke from his dream with a 'distinct recollection' and 'eagerly wrote down the lines that are here preserved', before he was interrupted by 'a person on business from Porlock'. On returning to his writing an hour later, however, he found that his trance had been broken.

In Xanadu did Kubla Khan
A stately pleasure-dome decree:
Where Alph, the sacred river, ran
Through caverns measureless to man
   Down to a sunless sea.
So twice five miles of fertile ground
With walls and towers were girdled round;
And there were gardens bright with sinuous rills,
Where blossomed many an incense-bearing tree;
And here were forests ancient as the hills,
Enfolding sunny spots of greenery.

But oh! that deep romantic chasm which slanted
Down the green hill athwart a cedarn cover!
A savage place! as holy and enchanted
As e'er beneath a waning moon was haunted
By woman wailing for her demon-lover!
And from this chasm, with ceaseless turmoil seething,
As if this earth in fast thick pants were breathing,
A mighty fountain momently was forced:
Amid whose swift half-intermitted burst

Huge fragments vaulted like rebounding hail,
Or chaffy grain beneath the thresher's flail:
And 'mid these dancing rocks at once and ever
It flung up momently the sacred river.
Five miles meandering with a mazy motion
Through wood and dale the sacred river ran,
Then reached the caverns measureless to man,
And sank in tumult to a lifeless ocean;
And 'mid this tumult Kubla heard from far
Ancestral voices prophesying war!
   The shadow of the dome of pleasure
   Floated midway on the waves;
   Where was heard the mingled measure
   From the fountain and the caves.
It was a miracle of rare device,
A sunny pleasure-dome with caves of ice!

   A damsel with a dulcimer
   In a vision once I saw:
   It was an Abyssinian maid
   And on her dulcimer she played,
   Singing of Mount Abora.
   Could I revive within me
   Her symphony and song,
   To such a deep delight 'twould win me,
That with music loud and long,
I would build that dome in air,
That sunny dome! those caves of ice!
And all who heard should see them there,
And all should cry, Beware! Beware!
His flashing eyes, his floating hair!
Weave a circle round him thrice,
And close your eyes with holy dread
For he on honey-dew hath fed,
And drunk the milk of Paradise.

12 October · Lament of an Arawak Child · Pamela Mordecai

On 12 October 1492, Christopher Columbus landed on the continent now known as America. Though he described the continent as his 'discovery', he was far from the first person to step foot there. In poetry, as in common usage, a 'lament' is an outpouring of grief. Mordecai's poem refuses to focus on what Columbus and other colonial figures thought they had found, but instead gives voice to the people who lost what they once had.

Once I played with the hummingbirds
and sang songs to the sea
I told my secrets to the waves
and they told theirs to me.

Now there are no more hummingbirds
the sea's songs are all sad
for strange men came and took this land
and plundered all we had.

They made my people into slaves
they worked us to the bone
they battered us and tortured us
and laughed to hear us groan.

Today we'll take a long canoe
and set sail on the sea
we'll steer our journey by the stars
and find a new country.

12 October · Ozymandias ·
Percy Bysshe Shelley

Similarly to Coleridge's 'Kubla Khan', Percy Bysshe
Shelley's sonnet 'Ozymandias' takes as its subject a
fantastical place in a distant land. The poem is the
result of a sonnet competition between Shelley and
his friend Horace Smith. They both wrote on the same
topic: a huge ruined statue in Egypt.

I met a traveller from an antique land,
Who said: 'Two vast and trunkless legs of stone
Stand in the desert . . . Near them, on the sand,
Half sunk, a shattered visage lies, whose frown,
And wrinkled lip, and sneer of cold command,
Tell that its sculptor well those passions read
Which yet survive, stamped on these lifeless things,
The hand that mocked them, and the heart that fed;
And on the pedestal, these words appear:
'My name is Ozymandias, king of kings;
Look on my works, ye Mighty, and despair!'
Nothing beside remains. Round the decay
Of that colossal wreck, boundless and bare
The lone and level sands stretch far away.

13 October · The Wild Swans at Coole · W. B. Yeats

Yeats's poem, about watching swans one October evening, gives quiet expression to time, change, and ageing. The narrator counts his passing years, but the swans, he suspects, do not. His worry, at the end of the poem, is that he will one day wake up and find that beauty has left his life for good.

The trees are in their autumn beauty,
The woodland paths are dry,
Under the October twilight the water
Mirrors a still sky;
Upon the brimming water among the stones
Are nine-and-fifty swans.

The nineteenth autumn has come upon me
Since I first made my count;
I saw, before I had well finished,
All suddenly mount
And scatter wheeling in great broken rings
Upon their clamorous wings.

I have looked upon those brilliant creatures,
And now my heart is sore.
All's changed since I, hearing at twilight,
The first time on this shore,
The bell-beat of their wings above my head,
Trod with a lighter tread.

Unwearied still, lover by lover,
They paddle in the cold
Companionable streams or climb the air;
Their hearts have not grown old;
Passion or conquest, wander where they will,
Attend upon them still.

But now they drift on the still water,
Mysterious, beautiful;
Among what rushes will they build,
By what lake's edge or pool
Delight men's eyes when I awake some day
To find they have flown away?

13 October · To Autumn · John Keats

In 1819 John Keats wrote a celebrated series of odes, now regarded as some of the finest poetry in the English language, the last of which is 'To Autumn'. The 'ode' is a poetic form in which a particular subject is discussed and celebrated – alongside his ode to Autumn, Keats took as his subjects the goddess Psyche, a nightingale, a Grecian urn, and the emotion melancholy.

Season of mists and mellow fruitfulness,
   Close bosom-friend of the maturing sun;
Conspiring with him how to load and bless
   With fruit the vines that round the thatch-eves run;
To bend with apples the moss'd cottage-trees,
   And fill all fruit with ripeness to the core;
     To swell the gourd, and plump the hazel shells
   With a sweet kernel; to set budding more,
And still more, later flowers for the bees,
Until they think warm days will never cease,
     For summer has o'er-brimm'd their clammy cells.

Who hath not seen thee oft amid thy store?
Sometimes whoever seeks abroad may find
Thee sitting careless on a granary floor,
Thy hair soft-lifted by the winnowing wind;
Or on a half-reap'd furrow sound asleep,
Drows'd with the fume of poppies, while thy hook
Spares the next swath and all its twined flowers:
And sometimes like a gleaner thou dost keep
Steady thy laden head across a brook;
Or by a cyder-press, with patient look,
Thou watchest the last oozings hours by hours.

Where are the songs of Spring? Ay, where are they?
Think not of them, thou hast thy music too,—
While barred clouds bloom the soft-dying day,
And touch the stubble-plains with rosy hue;
Then in a wailful choir the small gnats mourn
Among the river sallows, borne aloft
Or sinking as the light wind lives or dies;
And full-grown lambs loud bleat from hilly bourn;
Hedge-crickets sing; and now with treble soft
The red-breast whistles from a garden-croft;
And gathering swallows twitter in the skies.

14 October · William the Conqueror, 1066 · Anon.

The Battle of Hastings was a day-long battle that occurred on 14 October 1066 between the Anglo-Saxon English and the Norman army, who were invading. The Normans were victorious, and William, the Duke of Normandy – also known as William the Conqueror – was crowned King William I of England ten weeks later. These lines, a traditional and anonymous verse on the exploits of William, suggest that the only thing that ultimately stopped the Duke taking more territories for himself was his death.

William the Conqueror, 1066,
Said to his captains, 'I mean to affix
England to Normandy. Go out and borrow
Some bows and some arrows, we're starting tomorrow.'
So William went conquering hither and thither
'Til Angles and Saxons were all of a dither.
He conquered so quickly you couldn't keep count
Of the counties he conquered, I think they amount
To ten, or a doxen, or even a score,
And I haven't a doubt he'd have conquered some more,
But death put an end to the tactics, thanks Heaven,
Of William the Conqueror, 1087.

☾ 14 October · Anglo-Saxon riddle · Anon.

The Anglo-Saxons, a people who inhabited Great Britain from the fifth century and who dominated the country until the Norman Conquest of 1066, loved telling each other riddles. They had a rich literary tradition, and perhaps the most well-known work from the Anglo-Saxon period is the epic poem *Beowulf*, written in Old English, the ancient ancestor of the language we speak today. This riddle transforms a thing that we don't usually think of as a person into a 'wonderful warrior' with a fickle personality – and the solution to this puzzle is something both beautiful and extremely dangerous!

A wonderful warrior exists on earth.
Two dumb creatures make him grow bright between
   them.
Enemies use him against one another.
His strength is fierce but a woman can tame him.
He will meekly serve both men and women
If they know the trick of looking after him
And feeding him properly.
He makes people happy.
He makes their lives better.
But if they let him grow proud
This ungrateful friend soon turns against them.

The answer, if you have not guessed it, is fire!

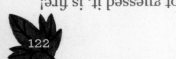

15 October · At Senlac Hill, 15 October 1066 · David Harmer

Following on from the anniversary of the Battle of Hastings, this is a poem named after the hill on which the Anglo-Saxon army was deployed at the start of the battle.

Broken blades still bright with blood
fallen and flung far over the field,
the battered bodies of mangled men,
beaten by battle, bruised and bleeding
crying for care, or still as stones
their shields shattered, their spears scattered
their breathing butchered, spent and stopped,
lie heaped and piled in many mounds.

My sister and I searched for our father
killed or captured, we don't know
but missing since midnight,
like Harold our King, now carrion crows
swoop and swirl over the fallen
pecking for pickings, our mother moans
weeps in her hands and holds her hair
away from her face, missing her man
amongst the many, the stiff and the still
or those who groan from their war-wounds.

Yesterday we were Saxons, English and angry
ready for riot against her foes
now we are Normans, French and fatherless
dazed and despairing, lost with dead
already our masters make preparations
digging their ditches to raise their ramparts
our future is dreaded, dismal and dull
stretched out in front of us like a dark day.

15 October · A Shropshire Lad, XIII · A. E. Housman

This poem was published in A. E. Housman's *A Shropshire Lad* and, like many of the poems in that collection, it is narrated by a speaker looking back on his youth. Even though, on this occasion, he is only twenty two.

When I was one-and-twenty
 I heard a wise man say,
'Give crowns and pounds and guineas
 But not your heart away;
Give pearls away and rubies
 But keep your fancy free.'
But I was one-and-twenty,
 No use to talk to me.

When I was one-and-twenty
 I heard him say again,
'The heart out of the bosom
 Was never given in vain;
'Tis paid with sighs a plenty
 And sold for endless rue.'
And I am two-and-twenty,
 And oh, 'tis true, 'tis true.

16 October · Not Only · Brian Patten

This poem by the Liverpudlian writer Brian Patten pushes forward along a single track, a series of 'Nos', arriving at one emphatic 'But': the object of his affection.

Not only the leaf shivering with delight
No,
Not only the morning grass shrugging off the weight of
    frost
No,
Not only the wings of the crane fly consumed by fire
No,
Not only steam rising from the horse's back
No,
Not only the sound of the sunflower roaring
No,
Not only the golden spider spinning
No,
Not only the cathedral window deep inside the raindrop
No,
Not only the door opening at the back of the clouds
No,
Not only flakes of light settling like snow
No,
Not only the sky as blue and smooth as an egg
No,
Not only these things
No,
But without you none of these things

In this poem a simple Autumnal image is transformed
into a visual riddle. We cannot just read this poem – we
have to decipher it. Cummings breaks up each word of
his poem, placing fragments of words on separate lines.
With the longest line being the last ('iness'), reading
this poem is like watching a leaf drift down from a tree
before settling on the ground.

l (a

le
af
fa
ll

s)
one
l

iness

17 October · The Secret Song ·
Margaret Wise Brown

In this poem, the American writer Margaret Wise Brown
imagines the world that humans don't see.

Who saw the petals
drop from the rose?
I, said the spider,
But nobody knows.

Who saw the sunset
flash on a bird?
I, said the fish,
But nobody heard.

Who saw the fog
come over the sea?
I, said the sea pigeon,
Only me.

Who saw the first
green light of the sun?
I, said the night owl,
The only one.

Who saw the moss
creep over the stone?
I, said the grey fox,
All alone.

17 October • Spiderweb • Kay Ryan

Kay Ryan is an award-winning American poet who often writes short poems, avoiding the first-person 'I'. At first, this poem appears to be a detailed description of the spider's work as it weaves its web, encouraging the reader to inhabit the spider's mind, rather than the human's. The final two sentences of the poem, however, move the focus of the poem outwards, drawing out a similarity between life of all kinds.

From other
angles the
fibers look
fragile, but
not from the
spider's, always
hauling coarse
ropes, hitching
lines to the
best posts
possible. It's
heavy work
everyplace,
fighting sag,
winching up
give. It
isn't ever
delicate
to live.

18 October · *from* Who Do You Think You Are? · Carl Sandburg

The question that makes up the title of this poem is a good one: when it really comes down to it, who do you think you are? Sandburg's answer to this question is comically, and quite obsessively to catalogue every last speck of substance that makes up a living human body.

> Who do you think you are
> and where do you think you came from?

From toenails to the hair of your head you are mixed of the earth, of the air,

Of compounds equal to the burning gold and amethyst lights of the Mountains of the Blood of Christ at Santa Fé.

Listen to the laboratory man tell you what you are made of, man, listen while he takes you apart.

Weighing 150 pounds you hold 3,500 cubic feet of gas — oxygen, hydrogen, nitrogen.

From the 22 pounds and 10 ounces of carbon in you is the filling for 9,000 lead pencils.

In your blood are 50 grains of iron and in the rest of your frame enough iron to make a spike that would hold your weight.

From your 50 ounces of phosphorus could be made 800,000 matches and elsewhere in your physical premises are hidden 60 lumps of sugar, 20 teaspoons of salt,

38 quarts of water, two ounces of lime, and scatterings of starch, chloride of potash, magnesium, sulphur, hydrochloric acid.
You are a walking drug store and also a cosmos and a phantasmagoria treading a lonesome valley, one of the people, one of the minions and myrmidons who would like an answer to the question, 'Who and what are you?'

The narrator of this poem is roused from his sleep by a knock at the door but, when he goes to answer, he realizes that there is nobody there. The descriptions of the natural world outside the door, however, suggests that the narrator is not really alone, as the nocturnal world is full of creatures.

Someone came knocking
At my wee, small door;
Someone came knocking;
I'm sure, sure, sure;
I listened, I opened,
I looked to left and right,
But nought there was a stirring
In the still dark night;
Only the busy beetle
Tap-tapping in the wall,
Only from the forest
The screech-owl's call,
Only the cricket whistling
While the dewdrops fall,
So I know not who came knocking,
At all, at all, at all.

19 October · Digging · Seamus Heaney

Heaney's poem, about his father and his grandfather at work digging, ends as a reflection on his own craft. He is not a skilled digger but a writer, with his squat pen acting as no replacement for a spade. But the poet recognizes that he is not, after all, his father nor his grandfather, and he will go to do the work he knows best, pen in hand.

Between my finger and my thumb
The squat pen rests; snug as a gun.

Under my window, a clean rasping sound
When the spade sinks into gravelly ground:
My father, digging. I look down

Till his straining rump among the flowerbeds
Bends low, comes up twenty years away
Stooping in rhythm through potato drills
Where he was digging.

The coarse boot nestled on the lug, the shaft
Against the inside knee was levered firmly.
He rooted out tall tops, buried the bright edge deep
To scatter new potatoes that we picked,
Loving their cool hardness in our hands.

By God, the old man could handle a spade.
Just like his old man.

My grandfather cut more turf in a day
Than any other man on Toner's bog.
Once I carried him milk in a bottle
Corked sloppily with paper. He straightened up

To drink it, then fell to right away
Nicking and slicing neatly, heaving sods
Over his shoulder, going down and down
For the good turf. Digging.

The cold smell of potato mould, the squelch and slap
Of soggy peat, the curt cuts of an edge
Through living roots awaken in my head.
But I've no spade to follow men like them.

Between my finger and my thumb
The squat pen rests.
I'll dig with it.

19 October · A Prayer for Travellers · Anon.

Gaelic is a Celtic language spoken in Ireland, and this is a traditional Irish Gaelic prayer. Celtic literature often uses natural imagery to illustrate God interacting with his people, as can be seen in this poem. 'May the road rise up to meet you' wishes travellers good luck for their upcoming journeys.

> May the road rise up to meet you.
> May the wind be always at your back.
> May the sun shine warm upon your face;
> The rains fall soft upon your fields.
> And until we meet again,
> May God hold you in the palm of His hand.

20 October · Diary of a Church Mouse · John Betjeman

Betjeman's verse makes observations about British culture, attitudes and behaviour, and this witty poem ends on a comment about people who only attend church on religious festivals, and not as a point of faith.

Here among long-discarded cassocks,
Damp stools, and half-split open hassocks,
Here where the Vicar never looks
I nibble through old service books.
Lean and alone I spend my days
Behind this Church of England baize.
I share my dark forgotten room
With two oil-lamps and half a broom.
The cleaner never bothers me,
So here I eat my frugal tea.
My bread is sawdust mixed with straw;
My jam is polish for the floor.
  Christmas and Easter may be feasts
For congregations and for priests,
And so may Whitsun. All the same,
They do not fill my meagre frame.
For me the only feast at all
Is Autumn's Harvest Festival,
When I can satisfy my want
With ears of corn around the font.
I climb the eagle's brazen head
To burrow through a loaf of bread.
I scramble up the pulpit stair
And gnaw the marrows hanging there.
  It is enjoyable to taste
These items ere they go to waste,

But how annoying when one finds
That other mice with pagan minds
Come into church my food to share
Who have no proper business there.
Two field mice who have no desire
To be baptized, invade the choir.
A large and most unfriendly rat
Comes in to see what we are at.
He says he thinks there is no God
And yet he comes . . . it's rather odd.
This year he stole a sheaf of wheat
(It screened our special preacher's seat),
And prosperous mice from fields away
Come in to hear the organ play,
And under cover of its notes
Ate through the altar's sheaf of oats.
A Low Church mouse, who thinks that I
Am too papistical, and High,
Yet somehow doesn't think it wrong
To munch through Harvest Evensong,
While I, who starve the whole year through,
Must share my food with rodents who
Except at this time of the year
Not once inside the church appear.
  Within the human world I know
Such goings-on could not be so,
For human beings only do
What their religion tells them to.
They read the Bible every day
And always, night and morning, pray,
And just like me, the good church mouse,
Worship each week in God's own house.
  But all the same it's strange to me
How very full the church can be
With people I don't see at all
Except at Harvest Festival.

☾ 20 October · The Guest House · Rumi, translated by Reynold A. Nicholson

In this poem it almost sounds as if the thirteenth-century Persian poet Rumi is telling his readers to embrace dark thoughts, shame and malice. But what he is really saying is to 'invite them in'; don't ignore your feelings. They may be of some higher significance.

This being human is a guest house,
Every morning a new arrival.

A joy, a depression, a meanness,
some momentary awareness comes
as an unexpected visitor.

Welcome and entertain them all!
Even if they are a crowd of sorrows,
who violently sweep your house
empty of its furniture,
still treat each guest honourably.
He may be clearing you out for some new delight.

The dark thought, the shame, the malice,
meet them at the door laughing,
and invite them in.

Be grateful for whoever comes,
because each has been sent
as a guide from beyond.

21 October · *from* The Battle of Trafalgar · William King

The Battle of Trafalgar was a naval battle fought between British forces and the combined navies of Spain and France on 21 October 1805. Before the battle, the commander of the British Navy, Admiral Horatio Nelson, sent a terse communication to his forces: 'England expects that every man will do his duty'. Though Nelson was killed during the battle, the outcome was a resounding victory for the British, who destroyed the French and Spanish forces without losing a ship.

The last great signal Nelson did unfold,
Albion, record! in characters of gold!
'England expects that ev'ry man this day,
Will do his duty and his worth display.'
Warm'd at the words, brave Nelson's gallant crew
Mow'd down whole hosts! and heaps of heroes slew;
Like grateful sons – obeyed their gallant chief
Whilst the lost hero filled their souls with grief.

Thomas Hardy

In the aftermath of the Battle of Trafalgar, Nelson was commemorated with a statue atop a column in London's Trafalgar Square, as well as in this poem by Thomas Hardy.

I

In the wild October night-time, when the wind raved
   round the land,
And the Back-sea met the Front-sea, and our doors were
   blocked with sand,
And we heard the drub of Dead-man's Bay, where the
   bones of thousands are,
We knew not what the day had done for us at Trafalgár.
        Had done,
        Had done,
     For us at Trafalgár!

II

'Pull hard, and make the Nothe, or down we go!' one
   says, says he.
We pulled; and bedtime brought the storm; but snug at
   home slept we.
Yet all the while our gallants after fighting through the
   day,
Were beating up and down the dark, sou'-west of Cadiz
   Bay.
           The dark,
           The dark,
         Sou'-west of Cadiz Bay!

III

The victors and the vanquished then the storm it tossed
   and tore,
As hard they strove, those worn-out men, upon that
   surly shore;
Dead Nelson and his half-dead crew, his foes from near
   and far,
Were rolled together on the deep that night at Trafalgár!
           The deep,
           The deep,
        That night at Trafalgár!

22 October · The Village Blacksmith · Henry Wadsworth Longfellow

According to Longfellow, this poem about working-class life was written as a tribute to an ancestor of his, a blacksmith named Stephen Longfellow. The man in the poem, however, was also modelled on a real blacksmith, a neighbour of the poet's. Longfellow transforms his life into a moral tale of decent living and of honest, hard work.

Under a spreading chestnut-tree
　The village smithy stands;
The smith, a mighty man is he,
　With large and sinewy hands;
And the muscles of his brawny arms
　Are strong as iron bands.

His hair is crisp, and black, and long,
　His face is like the tan;
His brow is wet with honest sweat,
　He earns whate'er he can,
And looks the whole world in the face,
　For he owes not any man.

Week in, week out, from morn till night,
　You can hear his bellows blow;
You can hear him swing his heavy sledge,
　With measured beat and slow,
Like a sexton ringing the village bell,
　When the evening sun is low.

And children coming home from school
   Look in at the open door;
They love to see the flaming forge,
   And hear the bellows roar,
And catch the burning sparks that fly
   Like chaff from a threshing-floor.

He goes on Sunday to the church,
   And sits among his boys;
He hears the parson pray and preach,
   He hears his daughter's voice,
Singing in the village choir,
   And it makes his heart rejoice.

It sounds to him like her mother's voice,
   Singing in Paradise!
He needs must think of her once more,
   How in the grave she lies;
And with his hard, rough hand he wipes
   A tear out of his eyes.

Toiling, – rejoicing, – sorrowing,
   Onward through life he goes;
Each morning sees some task begin,
   Each evening sees it close;
Something attempted, something done,
   Has earned a night's repose.

Thanks, thanks to thee, my worthy friend,
   For the lesson thou hast taught!
Thus at the flaming forge of life
   Our fortunes must be wrought;
Thus on its sounding anvil shaped
   Each burning deed and thought.

143

22 October · Inscription on the Monument of a Newfoundland Dog · George Gordon, Lord Byron

Dogs are often said to be 'man's best friend'. Lord Byron wrote this poem as an epitaph to his Newfoundland, Boatswain, and it can be found inscribed on the dog's tomb at Newstead Abbey, Byron's estate. Even though Boatswain died of rabies, which is highly infectious, reports from the time record that Byron nursed him personally until his death.

When some proud son of man returns to earth,
Unknown to glory but upheld by birth,
The sculptor's art exhausts the pomp of woe,
And storied urns record who rests below:
When all is done, upon the tomb is seen
Not what he was, but what he should have been.
But the poor dog, in life the firmest friend,
The first to welcome, foremost to defend,
Whose honest heart is still his master's own,
Who labours, fights, lives, breathes for him alone,
Unhonour'd falls, unnotic'd all his worth,
Denied in heaven the soul he held on earth,
While man, vain insect! hopes to be forgiven,
And claims himself a sole exclusive heaven.
Oh man! thou feeble tenant of an hour,
Debas'd by slavery, or corrupt by power,
Who knows thee well, must quit thee with disgust,
Degraded mass of animated dust!
Thy love is lust, thy friendship all a cheat,

Thy smiles hypocrisy, thy words deceit!
By nature vile, ennobled but by name,
Each kindred brute might bid thee blush for shame.
Ye! who behold perchance this simple urn,
Pass on – it honours none you wish to mourn.
To mark a friend's remains these stones arise;
I never knew but one – and here he lies.

23 October · A Country Boy Goes to School · George Mackay Brown

In this poem about school life, the Scottish poet George Mackay Brown plays off Romantic ideals with poetic reality. Specifically, he quotes the poet Wordsworth, who wrote 'Let Nature be your teacher'. The schoolboy wants to follow this course of education by listening to the lark, but instead winds up in trouble with his real teacher.

1

There he is, first lark this year
   Loud, between
That raincloud and the sun, lost
Up there, a long sky run, what peltings of song!
   (Six times 6, 36. Six times 7, 42
   Six times eight is . . .)
Oh, Mr Ferguson, have mercy at arithmetic time
   On peedie Tom o' the Glebe.

2

There's Gyre's ewe has 2 lambs.
   Snow on the ridge still.
How many more days do I have to take
This peat under my oxter
   For the school fire?
(James the Sixth, Charles the First . . . Who then?)
Oh, Mr Ferguson, I swear
   I knew all the Stewarts last night.

3

Yes, Mistress Wylie, we're all fine.
   A pandrop! Oh, thank you.
I must hurry, Mistress Wylie,
   Old Ferguson
Gets right mad if a boy's late.
I was late twice last week.
   Do you know this, Mistress Wylie,
The capital of Finland is Helsingfors . . .
   Yes, I'll tell Grannie
You have four fat feese this summer.

4

When I get to the top of the brae
I'll see the kirk, the school, the shop,
   Smithy and inn and boatyard.
I wish I was that tinker boy
Going on over the hill, the wind in his rags.

Look, the schoolyard's like a throng of bees.

5

I wish Willie Thomson
   Would take me on his creel-boat!
'Tom, there's been six generations of Corstons
   Working the Glebe,
And I doubt there'll never be fish-scales
On your hands, or salt in your boots . . .'

(Sixteen ounces, one pound. Fourteen pounds, one stone.)
A sack of corn's a hundredweight.
   I think a whale must be bigger than a ton.

6

Jimmo Spence, he told me
  Where the larks nest is.
  Besides a stone in his father's oatfield,
  The high granite corner.

('I wandered lonely as a cloud . . .' Oh where? What then?)
I could go up by the sheep track
  Now the scholars are in their pen
And *Scallop* and *Mayflower* are taking the flood
  And the woman of Fea
Is pinning her washing to the wind.

I could wait for the flutter of the lark coming down.

7

The school bell! Oh, my heart's
Pounding louder than any bell.

  A quarter of a mile to run.
  My bare feet
  Have broken three daffodils in the field.

Heart thunderings, last tremor of the bell
  And the lark wing-folded.

'Late again, Master Thomas Corston of the Glebe farm.
Enter, sir. With the greatest interest
  We all await your explanation
Of a third morning's dereliction.'

23 October · El Alamein · John Jarmain

During World War Two, on 23 October 1942, the Battle of El Alamein began in North Africa. The British commander Montgomery led the Eighth Army to victory over German Field Marshal Rommel's Afrika Korps, and it proved to be a turning point in the war in Africa. An army officer and a war poet, John Jarmain wrote this poem a year after fighting at El Alamein. Tragically he was killed by shrapnel in Normandy in June 1944, when he was just thirty-three.

There are flowers now, they say, at Alamein;
Yes, flowers in the minefields now.
So those that come to view that vacant scene,
Where death remains and agony has been
Will find the lilies grow –
Flowers, and nothing that we know.

So they rang the bells for us and Alamein,
Bells which we could not hear:
And to those that heard the bells, what could it mean,
That name of loss and pride, El Alamein?
– Not the murk and harm of war,
But their hope, their own warm prayer.

149

It will become a staid historic name,
That crazy sea of sand!
Like Troy or Agincourt its single fame
Will be the garland for our brow, our claim,
On us a fleck of glory to the end:
And there our dead will keep their holy ground.

But this is not the place that we recall,
The crowded desert crossed with foaming tracks,
The one blotched building, lacking half a wall,
The grey-faced men, sand powdered over all;
The tanks, the guns, the trucks,
The black, dark-smoking wrecks.

So be it: none but us has known that land:
El Alamein will still be only ours
And those ten days of chaos in the sand.
Others will come who cannot understand,
Will halt beside the rusty minefield wires
And find there – flowers.

24 October • Owl Poem • John Hegley

John Hegley is a British performance poet and comedian, and the author of many books. This 'poem' is actually four acrostic poems – poems which spell out a word with the first letters of their lines. Oh, wholeheartedly literary, our witty lyricist!

On
Wards
Lofty

Oh,
Winged
Looker

Out
Witting
Low-life

Ooooh
Wooooooo
Language

151

The Battle of Agincourt took place on 25 October 1415 and serves as the central set-piece of Shakespeare's historical drama Henry V. This short prologue to the fourth act describes the last minute preparations and the anxious atmosphere in the English camp the night before the conflict. As the soldiers sit shrouded by fear of imminent death, the young king goes around reassuring his nervous troops with 'a little touch of Harry' — the unexpected colloquial nature of that phrase emphasising the monarch's solidarity with all his men.

> Now entertain conjecture of a time
> When creeping murmur and the poring dark
> Fills the wide vessel of the universe.
> From camp to camp through the foul womb of night
> The hum of either army stilly sounds,
> That the fixed sentinels almost receive
> The secret whispers of each other's watch:
> Fire answers fire, and through their paly flames
> Each battle sees the other's umber'd face;
> Steed threatens steed, in high and boastful neighs
> Piercing the night's dull ear, and from the tents
> The armourers, accomplishing the knights,
> With busy hammers closing rivets up,
> Give dreadful note of preparation.
> The country cocks do crow, the clocks do toll,
> And the third hour of drowsy morning name.
> Proud of their numbers and secure in soul,
> The confident and over-lusty French

Do the low-rated English play at dice;
And chide the cripple tardy-gaited night
Who, like a foul and ugly witch, doth limp
So tediously away. The poor condemnèd English,
Like sacrifices, by their watchful fires
Sit patiently and inly ruminate
The morning's danger, and their gesture sad,
Investing lank-lean cheeks and war-worn coats,
Presenteth them unto the gazing moon
So many horrid ghosts. O now, who will behold
The royal captain of this ruin'd band
Walking from watch to watch, from tent to tent,
Let him cry 'Praise and glory on his head!'
For forth he goes and visits all his host,
Bids them good morrow with a modest smile,
And calls them brothers, friends and countrymen.
Upon his royal face there is no note
How dread an army hath enrounded him;
Nor doth he dedicate one jot of colour
Unto the weary and all-watchèd night,
But freshly looks and over-bears attaint
With cheerful semblance and sweet majesty,
That every wretch, pining and pale before,
Beholding him, plucks comfort from his looks.
A largess universal, like the sun,
His liberal eye doth give to every one,
Thawing cold fear, that mean and gentle all
Behold, as may unworthiness define,
A little touch of Harry in the night.
And so our scene must to the battle fly;
Where – O for pity! – we shall much disgrace
With four or five most vile and ragged foils
Right ill-disposed in brawl ridiculous
The name of Agincourt.

25 October · *from* Henry V ·
William Shakespeare

Known as the 'St Crispin's Day speech', this stirring
address delivered by Henry V on the morning of the
Battle of Agincourt presents the conflict, not as a vain
pursuit of wealth and power, but as a matter of honour
and reputation – personal and national. The English
may be heavily outnumbered by the French, but Henry
galvanizes his men here by compelling them to see
themselves as a 'band of brothers'. The speech took on a
modern resonance during the Second World War, when
it was delivered rousingly by Laurence Olivier in his
1944 film adaptation of the play.

This day is called the feast of Crispian:
He that outlives this day, and comes safe home,
Will stand a tip-toe when the day is named,
And rouse him at the name of Crispian.
He that shall live this day, and see old age,
Will yearly on the vigil feast his neighbours,
And say, 'To-morrow is Saint Crispian.'
Then will he strip his sleeve and show his scars,
And say, 'These wounds I had on Crispin's day.'
Old men forget; yet all shall be forgot,
But he'll remember with advantages
What feats he did that day. Then shall our names,
Familiar in his mouth as household words –
Harry the King, Bedford and Exeter,
Warwick and Talbot, Salisbury and Gloucester –
Be in their flowing cups freshly remember'd.

This story shall the good man teach his son;
And Crispin Crispian shall ne'er go by,
From this day to the ending of the world,
But we in it shall be remembered;
We few, we happy few, we band of brothers;
For he today that sheds his blood with me
Shall be my brother; be he ne'er so vile,
This day shall gentle his condition;
And gentlemen in England now a-bed
Shall think themselves accursed they were not here,
And hold their manhoods cheap whiles any speaks
That fought with us upon Saint Crispin's day.

25 October · The Charge of the Light Brigade · Alfred, Lord Tennyson

Alfred, Lord Tennyson, wrote 'The Charge of the Light Brigade' after reading a newspaper account of the disastrous British cavalry charge against Russian forces at the Battle of Balaclava, which was fought on 25 October 1854. The ill-fated charge was the result of a miscommunication in the chain of command, and many of the 600 soldiers died.

> Half a league, half a league,
>   Half a league onward,
> All in the valley of Death
>   Rode the six hundred.
> 'Forward, the Light Brigade!
> Charge for the guns!' he said.
> Into the valley of Death
>   Rode the six hundred.
>
> 'Forward, the Light Brigade!'
> Was there a man dismayed?
> Not though the soldier knew
>   Someone had blundered.
> Theirs not to make reply,
> Theirs not to reason why,
> Theirs but to do and die.
> Into the valley of Death
>   Rode the six hundred.

Cannon to right of them,
Cannon to left of them,
Cannon in front of them
  Volleyed and thundered;
Stormed at with shot and shell,
Boldly they rode and well,
Into the jaws of Death,
Into the mouth of Hell
  Rode the six hundred.

Flashed all their sabres bare,
Flashed as they turned in air
Sabring the gunners there,
Charging an army, while
  All the world wondered.
Plunged in the battery-smoke
Right through the line they broke;
Cossack and Russian
Reeled from the sabre-stroke
  Shattered and sundered.
Then they rode back, but not
  Not the six hundred.

Cannon to right of them,
Cannon to left of them,
Cannon behind them
  Volleyed and thundered;
Stormed at with shot and shell,
While horse and hero fell.
They that had fought so well
Came through the jaws of Death,
Back from the mouth of Hell,
All that was left of them,
  Left of six hundred.

157

When can their glory fade?
O the wild charge they made!
  All the world wondered.
Honour the charge they made!
Honour the Light Brigade,
  Noble six hundred!

26 October · Love After Love · Derek Walcott

Born in St Lucia, Derek Walcott ranks amongst the finest of Caribbean poets. He died in 2017, leaving behind him a wealth of poems, plays and essays. His writings earned him the Nobel Prize for Literature in 1992. This poem is about learning to love yourself again after the end of a relationship.

The time will come
when, with elation
you will greet yourself arriving
at your own door, in your own mirror,
and each will smile at the other's welcome,

and say sit here. Eat.
You will love again the stranger who was your self,
Give wine. Give bread. Give back your heart
to itself, to the stranger who has loved you

all your life, whom you ignored
for another, who knows you by heart.
Take down the love-letters from the bookshelf

the photographs, the desperate notes,
peel your own image from the mirror.
Sit. Feast on your life.

159

26 October · *from* Auguries of Innocence ·
William Blake

Though 'Auguries of Innocence' is thought to have
been written in the first few years of the nineteenth
century, the poem was not published until 1866 – long
after William Blake had died. These four lines are
characteristically enigmatic of Blake: each line contains
a paradox, with a tiny grain of sand holding a world in
it, and eternity lasting just sixty minutes.

> To see a World in a Grain of Sand
> And a Heaven in a Wild Flower
> Hold Infinity in the palm of your hand
> And Eternity in an hour

27 October • Paper Boats • Rabindranath Tagore

Rabindranath Tagore was the recipient of the Nobel Prize for Literature in 1913, and was a noted artist and musician as well as a poet. He was born and lived in Calcutta in India for his entire life, which was then under British rule. This poem is about quietly attempting to make contact with the universe outside of yourself. The paper boats themselves act like Tagore's poems – he does not know to whom they will travel, nor what they will mean to his readers, but in his dreams they take on a life of their own.

Day by day I float my paper boats one by one down the
    running stream.
In big black letters I write my name on them and the
    name of the village where I live.
I hope that someone in some strange land will find them
    and know who I am.
I load my little boats with shiuli flowers from our
    garden, and hope that these blooms of the dawn will
    be carried safely to land in the night.
I launch my paper boats and look into the sky and see
    the little clouds setting their white bulging sails.
I know not what playmate of mine in the sky sends
    them down the air to race with my boats!
When night comes I bury my face in my arms and
    dream that my paper boats float on and on under the
    midnight stars.
The fairies of sleep are sailing in them, and the lading is
    their baskets full of dreams.

161

27 October · *from* Song Of Myself ·
Walt Whitman

In this extract from his sprawling masterpiece 'Song of Myself', Whitman begins by extolling the virtues of the natural world, arguing that even a single blade of grass or an ant is as beautiful and meaningful as anything in the universe – and certainly more impressive than man-made objects. The narrator is so devoted to immersing himself in nature, that nothing, no retreating waves or hiding animals, can deter him from taking it all in. At the end he reflects on this landscape from above, having already provided the reader with a similarly all-encompassing view with his words.

I believe a leaf of grass is no less than the journey-work
    of the stars,
And the pismire is equally perfect, and a grain of sand,
    and the egg of the wren,
And the tree-toad is a chef-d'oeuvre for the highest,
And the running blackberry would adorn the parlors of
    heaven,
And the narrowest hinge in my hand puts to scorn all
    machinery,
And the cow crunching with depress'd head surpasses
    any statue,
And a mouse is miracle enough to stagger sextillions of
    infidels.

I find I incorporate gneiss, coal, long-threaded moss,
    fruits, grains, esculent roots,
And am stucco'd with quadrupeds and birds all over,
And have distanced what is behind me for good reasons,
But call any thing back again when I desire it.
In vain the speeding or shyness,
In vain the plutonic rocks send their old heat against my
    approach,
In vain the mastodon retreats beneath its own powder'd
    bones,
In vain objects stand leagues off and assume manifold
    shapes,
In vain the ocean settling in hollows and the great
    monsters lying low,
In vain the buzzard houses herself with the sky,
In vain the snake slides through the creepers and logs,
In vain the elk takes to the inner passes of the woods,
In vain the razor-bill'd auk sails far north to Labrador,
I follow quickly, I ascend to the nest in the fissure of the
    cliff.

28 October · The New Colossus · Emma Lazarus

On 28 October 1886 an official ceremony of dedication marked the opening of the Statue of Liberty – a gift from the people of France to America. One of the most instantly recognizable symbols of America, the statue depicts the robed Roman goddess Libertas, the embodiment of liberty. The American poet Emma Lazarus wrote her sonnet 'The New Colossus' in 1883. The poem was engraved on a bronze plaque and mounted on the pedestal of the statue in 1903.

Not like the brazen giant of Greek fame,
With conquering limbs astride from land to land;
Here at our sea-washed, sunset gates shall stand
A mighty woman with a torch, whose flame
Is the imprisoned lightning, and her name
Mother of Exiles. From her beacon-hand
Glows world-wide welcome; her mild eyes command
The air-bridged harbor that twin cities frame.
'Keep, ancient lands, your storied pomp!' cries she
With silent lips. 'Give me your tired, your poor,
Your huddled masses yearning to breathe free,
The wretched refuse of your teeming shore.
Send these, the homeless, tempest-tost to me,
I lift my lamp beside the golden door!'

28 October · Western Wind, When Wilt Thou Blow? · Anon.

These lyrics are part of a song written in the early sixteenth century, though they probably have their roots in medieval poetry. The words are designed to be chanted, and connect written poems to the oral history of poetry. Before poems were written down, they were sung and repeated, and passed from person to person, much like we still do today with nursery rhymes and football chants!

> Western wind, when wilt thou blow,
> The small rain down can rain?
> Christ, if my love were in my arms
> And I in my bed again.

29 October · Who Has Seen the Wind? ·
Christina Rossetti

From Western Wind to the wind in this poem by
Rossetti. These deceptively simple words communicate
a sense of the invisible forces that animate the world —
forces which we cannot see, but we know must be there.

Who has seen the wind?
 Neither I nor you:
But when the leaves hang trembling,
 The wind is passing thro'.

Who has seen the wind?
 Neither you nor I:
But when the trees bow down their heads,
 The wind is passing by.

29 October · Leaves · Ted Hughes

In this poem, Ted Hughes puts an original twist on the traditional pastoral theme of the changing of the seasons, as he documents the process of Summer turning into Autumn, and then Winter, through the journey of the leaves. Throughout the piece, every aspect of the natural world is personified, from the trees to the whistling wind.

Who's killed the leaves?
Me, says the apple, I've killed them all.
Fat as a bomb or a cannonball
I've killed the leaves.

Who sees them drop?
Me, says the pear, they will leave me all bare
So all the people can point and stare.
I see them drop.

Who'll catch their blood?
Me, me, me, says the marrow, the marrow.
I'll get so rotund that they'll need a wheelbarrow.
I'll catch their blood.

Who'll make their shroud?
Me, says the swallow, there's just time enough
Before I must pack all my spools and be off.
I'll make their shroud.

Who'll dig their grave?
Me, says the river, with the power of the clouds
A brown deep grave I'll dig under my floods.
I'll dig their grave.

Who'll be their parson?
Me, says the Crow, for it is well known
I study the bible right down to the bone.
I'll be their parson.

Who'll be chief mourner?
Me, says the wind, I will cry through the grass
The people will pale and go cold when I pass.
I'll be chief mourner.

Who'll carry the coffin?
Me, says the sunset, the whole world will weep
To see me lower it into the deep.
I'll carry the coffin.

Who'll sing a psalm?
Me, says the tractor, with my gear-grinding glottle
I'll plough up the stubble and sing through my throttle.
I'll sing the psalm.

Who'll toll the bell?
Me, says the robin, my song in October
Will tell the still gardens the leaves are over.
I'll toll the bell.

30 October • A Boxing We Will Go • Anon.

On 30 October 1974, Muhammad Ali, whom many call the greatest sportsman of all time, fought the fight of his life and knocked out the then heavyweight boxing champion of the world, George Foreman. The event's name was the Rumble in the Jungle, and it took place in Zaire (now the Democratic Republic of the Congo). This nineteenth-century poem talks about the importance of boxing in Great Britain and names the three star boxers of the time. All of them would stand up to Boney, better known as Napoleon Bonaparte.

Throw pistols, poniards, swords aside,
And all such deadly tools;
Let boxing be the Briton's pride,
The science of their schools.
Since boxing is a manly game,
And Briton's recreation;
By boxing we will raise our fame,
'Bove any other nation
Mendoza, Bully, Molineux
Each nature's weapon wield;
Who each at Boney would stand true,
And never to him yield.

☾ 30 October · In the Dark, Dark Wood · Anon.

This is the perfect poem for the run up to Hallowe'en. When read aloud, the repetition builds tension through the poem up to the last word, which will make your audience jump!

In a dark, dark wood there was a dark, dark house,
and in that dark, dark house there was a dark, dark
  room,
and in that dark, dark room there was a dark, dark
  cupboard,
and in that dark, dark cupboard there was a dark, dark
  shelf,
and on that dark, dark shelf there was a dark, dark box,
and in that dark, dark box there was a . . . *GHOST*!

31 October · *from* Hallowe'en ·
John Kendrick Bangs

Today is All Hallows' Eve or All Saints' Eve, better
known as Hallowe'en. It is a time for remembering the
dead, but it is also, in popular culture, a time for raising
the dead: Hallowe'en is, of course, associated with
ghosts, ghouls and ghastly monsters. These words by
the American poet John Kendrick Bangs are a tribute to
Hallowe'en as we recognize it today.

> The ghosts of all things, past parade,
> Emerging from the mist and shade
> That hid them from our gaze,
> And full of song and ringing mirth,
> In one glad moment of rebirth,
> Again they walk the ways of earth,
> As in the ancient days.
>
> The beacon light shines on the hill,
> The will-o'-wisps the forests fill
> With flashes filched from noon;
> And witches on their broomsticks spry
> Speed here and yonder in the sky,
> And lift their strident voices high
> Unto the Hunter's moon.
>
> The air resounds with tuneful notes
> From myriads of straining throats,
> All hailing Folly Queen;
> So join the swelling choral throng,
> Forget your sorrow and your wrong,
> In one glad hour of joyous song
> To honor Hallowe'en.

☾ **31 October** · Down Vith Children! · Roald Dahl

The tradition of dressing up for Hallowe'en dates back to at least the sixteenth century. While we dress up on Hallowe'en to look terrifying, the evil witches of Roald Dahl's poem, taken from his book *The Witches*, have to dress up to look like humans – underneath their daily disguises they are truly gruesome!

Down vith children! Do them in!
Boil their bones and fry their skin!
Bish them, sqvish them, bash them, mash them!
Brrreak them, shake them, slash them, smash them!
Offer chocs vith magic powder!
Say, 'Eat up!' then say it louder.
Crrram them full of sticky eats,
Send them home still guzzling sveets.
And in the morning little fools
Go marching off to separate schools.
A girl feels sick and goes all pale.
She yells, 'Hey look! I've grrrown a tail!'
A boy who's standing next to her
Screams, 'Help! I think I'm grrrowing fur!'
Another shouts, 'Vee look like frrreaks!
There's viskers growing on our cheeks!'
A boy who vos extremely tall
Cries out, 'Vot's wrong? I'm grrrowing small!'
Four tiny legs begin to sprrrout
From everybody rrround about.
And all at vunce, all in a trrrice,
There are no children! Only MICE!

In every school is mice galore
All rrrunning rrround the school-rrroom floor!
And all the poor demented teachers
Is yelling, 'Hey, who are these crrreatures?'
They stand upon the desks and shout,
'Get out, you filthy mice! Get out!
Vill someone fetch some mouse-trrraps, please!
And don't forrrget to bring the cheese!'
Now mouse-trrraps come and every trrrap
Goes snippy-snip and snappy-snap.
The mouse-trrraps have a powerful spring,
The springs go crack and snap and ping!
Is lovely noise for us to hear!
Is music to a vitch's ear!
Dead mice is every place arrround,
Piled two feet deep upon the grrround,
Vith teachers searching left and rrright,
But not a single child in sight!
The teachers cry, 'Vot's going on?
Oh vhere have all the children gone?
Is half-past nine and as a rrrule
They're never late as this for school!'
Poor teachers don't know vot to do.
Some sit and rrread, and just a few
Amuse themselves throughout the day
By sveeping all the mice avay.
AND ALL US VITCHES SHOUT 'HOORAY!'

173

November

1 November · No! · Thomas Hood

Thomas Hood was a nineteenth-century English author, poet and humorist. This poem is an example of a kind of extended pun, as Hood's list of phrases beginning with 'no' is revealed by the final line to be a list of all the negative characteristics of the month of November.

No sun—no moon!
    No morn—no noon—
No dawn—no dusk—no proper time of day.
No warmth, no cheerfulness, no healthful ease,
  No comfortable feel in any member—
  No shade, no shine, no butterflies, no bees,
    No fruits, no flowers, no leaves, no birds,
        November!

1 November · *from* The Devil's Thoughts · Samuel Taylor Coleridge

November 1 is All Saints' Day or All Hallows Day (which follows All Hallows Eve or Hallowe'en). This witty poem, by Samuel Taylor Coleridge with some help from his friend, the lesser known Romantic poet Robert Southey, sees the devil take a tour of late eighteenth-century England – and he finds kindred spirits among lawyers and booksellers alike. In notes that appeared under the printed poem, Coleridge explained that he was indebted to 'that most interesting of the Devil's biographers', John Milton, author of *Paradise Lost*.

From his brimstone bed at break of day
A walking the Devil is gone,
To visit his little snug farm the earth,
And see how his stock goes on.

Over the hill and over the dale,
And he went over the plain,
And backward and forward he switched his long tail
As a gentleman switches his cane.

And how then was the Devil drest?
Oh! he was in his Sunday's best:
His jacket was red and his breeches were blue,
And there was a hole where the tail came through.

2 **November** · *from* Macbeth ·
William Shakespeare

November 2 is All Soul's Day and an opportunity
for Catholics to pray for all the souls who are in
purgatory. This passage is taken from Act 4, Scene 1 of
Shakespeare's *Macbeth*, one of his darkest and most
famous tragedies. The mysterious witches who have
prophesied Macbeth's ascent to the throne of Scotland
chant this haunting rhyme while brewing a potion.
Their spells and prophecies cause Macbeth more harm
than good, for at the end of the play both the villainous
Macbeth and his power-hungry wife suffer grisly fates.
This passage is a particularly good one to learn off by
heart – it's filled with memorable rhymes and catchy
alliteration.

> Double, double, toil and trouble;
> Fire burn, and cauldron bubble.
>
> Fillet of a fenny snake,
> In the cauldron boil and bake;
> Eye of newt and toe of frog,
> Wool of bat and tongue of dog,
> Adder's fork and blind-worm's sting,
> Lizard's leg and owlet's wing,
> For a charm of powerful trouble,
> Like a hell-broth boil and bubble.
>
> Double, double, toil and trouble;
> Fire burn, and cauldron bubble.

Scale of dragon, tooth of wolf,
Witches' mummy, maw and gulf
Of the ravin'd salt-sea shark,
Root of hemlock digg'd i' the dark,
Scale of dragon, tooth of wolf,
Witches' mummy, maw and gulf
Of the ravin'd salt-sea shark,
Root of hemlock digg'd i' the dark,
Add thereto a tiger's chaudron,
For the ingredients of our cauldron.

Double, double, toil and trouble;
Fire burn and cauldron bubble.

2 November · Television · Roald Dahl

The world's first high-definition television broadcast took place on this day in 1936, when BBC engineers set up a transmission mast at London's Alexandra Palace utilizing technology designed by John Logie Baird. Here is Roald Dahl's inimitable take on TV from *Charlie and the Chocolate Factory*.

The most important thing we've learned,
So far as children are concerned,
Is never, *NEVER*, NEVER let
Them near your television set –
Or better still, just don't install
The idiotic thing at all.
In almost every house we've been,
We've watched them gaping at the screen.
They loll and slop and lounge about,
And stare until their eyes pop out.
(Last week in someone's place we saw
A dozen eyeballs on the floor.)
They sit and stare and stare and sit
Until they're hypnotized by it,
Until they're absolutely drunk
With all that shocking ghastly junk.
Oh yes, we know it keeps them still,
They don't climb out the window sill,
They never fight or kick or punch,
They leave you free to cook the lunch
And wash the dishes in the sink –
But did you ever stop to think,
To wonder just exactly what
This does to your beloved tot?

IT ROTS THE SENSE IN THE HEAD!
IT KILLS IMAGINATION DEAD!
IT CLOGS AND CLUTTERS UP THE MIND!
IT MAKES A CHILD SO DULL AND BLIND
HE CAN NO LONGER UNDERSTAND
A FANTASY, A FAIRYLAND!
HIS BRAIN BECOMES AS SOFT AS CHEESE!
HIS POWERS OF THINKING RUST AND FREEZE!
HE CANNOT THINK – HE ONLY SEES!
'All right!' you'll cry. 'All right!' you'll say,
'But if we take the set away,
What shall we do to entertain
Our darling children? Please explain!'
We'll answer this by asking you,
'What used the darling ones to do?
How used they keep themselves contented
Before this monster was invented?'
Have you forgotten? Don't you know?
We'll say it very loud and slow:
THEY ... USED ... TO ... READ! They'd
   READ and READ,
AND READ and READ, and then proceed
TO READ some more. Great Scott! Gadzooks!
One half their lives was reading books!
The nursery shelves held books galore!
Books cluttered up the nursery floor!
And in the bedroom, by the bed,
More books were waiting to be read!
Such wondrous, fine, fantastic tales
Of dragons, gypsies, queens, and whales
And treasure isles, and distant shores
Where smugglers rowed with muffled oars,
And pirates wearing purple pants,
And sailing ships and elephants,
And cannibals crouching round the pot,

Stirring away at something hot.
(It smells so good, what can it be?
Good gracious, it's Penelope.)
The younger ones had Beatrix Potter
With Mr Tod, the dirty rotter,
And Squirrel Nutkin, Pigling Bland,
And Mrs Tiggy-Winkle and –
Just How The Camel Got His Hump,
And How the Monkey Lost His Rump,
And Mr Toad, and bless my soul,
There's Mr Rat and Mr Mole –
Oh, books, what books they used to know,
Those children living long ago!
So please, oh please, we beg, we pray,
Go throw your TV set away,
And in its place you can install
A lovely bookshelf on the wall.
Then fill the shelves with lots of books,
Ignoring all the dirty looks,
The screams and yells, the bites and kicks,
And children hitting you with sticks –
Fear not, because we promise you
That, in about a week or two
Of having nothing else to do,
They'll now begin to feel the need
Of having something good to read.
And once they start – oh boy, oh boy!
You watch the slowly growing joy
That fills their hearts. They'll grow so keen
They'll wonder what they'd ever seen
In that ridiculous machine,
That nauseating, foul, unclean,
Repulsive television screen!
And later, each and every kid
Will love you more for what you did.

3 November · The First Men on Mercury · Edwin Morgan

On this day in 1973, the NASA space probe Mariner 10 was launched from Cape Canaveral, with the goal of flying by the planets Mercury and Venus. After it successfully completed its missions, it was switched off on 24 March the following year. It is very likely still floating in a series of long orbits around the sun.

    — We come in peace from the third planet.
Would you take us to your leader?

    — Bawr stretter! Bawr. Bawr. Stretterhawl?

    — This is a little plastic model
of the solar system, with working parts.
You are here and we are there and we
are now here with you, is this clear?

    — Gawl horrop. Bawr Abawrhannahanna!

    — Where we come from is blue and white
with brown, you see we call the brown
here 'land', the blue is 'sea', and the white
is 'clouds' over land and sea, we live
on the surface of the brown land,
all round is sea and clouds. We are 'men'.
Men come —

    — Glawp men! Gawrbenner menko. Menhawl?

    — Men come in peace from the third planet
which we call 'earth'. We are earthmen.

Take us earthmen to your leader.

– Thmen? Thmen? Bawr. Bawrhossop.
Yuleeda tan hanna. Harrabost yuleeda.

– I am the yuleeda. You see my hands,
we carry no benner, we come in peace.
The spaceways are all stretterhawn.

– Glawn peacemen all horrabhanna tantko!
Tan come at'mstrossop. Glawp yuleeda!

– Atoms are peacegawl in our harraban.
Menbat worrabost from tan hannahanna.

– You men we know bawrhossoptant. Bawr.
We know yuleeda. Go strawg backspetter quick.

– We cantantabawr, tantingko backspetter now!

– Banghapper now! Yes, third planet back.
Yuleeda will go back blue, white, brown
nowhanna! There is no more talk.

– Gawl han fasthapper?

– No. You must go back to your planet.
Go back in peace, take what you have gained
but quickly.

– Stretterworra gawl, gawl . . .

– Of course, but nothing is ever the same,
now is it? You'll remember Mercury.

☾ 3 November • The Girl with Many Eyes • Tim Burton

The American Tim Burton is best known for his film-directing work that includes *The Nightmare Before Christmas* and film adaptations of Roald Dahl's *Charlie and the Chocolate Factory* and Lewis Carroll's *Alice in Wonderland*. He is also a writer and an artist, and much of his work reflects his quirky and fantastical imagination.

One day in the park,
I had quite a surprise.
I met a girl,
who had many eyes.

She was really quite pretty
(and also quite shocking)
and I noticed she had a mouth,
so we ended up talking.

We talked about flowers,
and her poetry classes,
and the problems she'd have
if she ever wore glasses.

It's great to know a girl
who has so many eyes,
but you get really wet
when she breaks down and cries.

4 **November** · The Last Laugh ·
Wilfred Owen

The war poet Wilfred Owen was killed in action on this day in 1918. He died exactly one week before Armistice Day, when hostilities finally ceased on the Western Front. His mother received a telegram with the news of his death the same day that Britain was celebrating peace in Europe. This poem, about a dying soldier in the trenches, is especially poignant in light of the poet's own death.

'O Jesus Christ! I'm hit,' he said; and died.
Whether he vainly cursed or prayed indeed,
       The Bullets chirped – In vain, vain, vain!
       Machine-guns chuckled – Tut-tut! Tut-tut!
       And the Big Gun guffawed.

Another sighed, – 'O Mother, – mother, – Dad!'
Then smiled at nothing, childlike, being dead.
       And the lofty Shrapnel-cloud
       Leisurely gestured, – Fool!
       And the splinters spat, and tittered.

'My Love!' one moaned. Love-languid seemed his mood,
Till slowly lowered, his whole face kissed the mud.
       And the Bayonets' long teeth grinned;
       Rabbles of Shells hooted and groaned;
       And the Gas hissed.

Wilfred Owen composed 'Dulce et Decorum Est' while
recovering from shell-shock in 1917. The title is taken
from a passage of Horace, the Roman poet, who wrote
that 'dulce et decorum est pro patria mori': 'it is sweet
and fitting to die for one's country.' While Horace
meant to praise the bravery of the Roman army, in
Owen's poem the phrase takes on a bitter irony. Owen's
descriptions of war are not lofty and idealized but
brutally graphic. He attacks the military propaganda
of the time which encouraged 'children ardent for
some desperate glory' to serve in the war, setting the
supposed sweetness of glory in battle in contrast with
the horrendous reality.

Bent double, like old beggars under sacks,
Knock-kneed, coughing like hags, we cursed through
    sludge,
Till on the haunting flares we turned our backs
And towards our distant rest began to trudge.
Men marched asleep. Many had lost their boots
But limped on, blood-shod. All went lame; all blind;
Drunk with fatigue; deaf even to the hoots
Of gas-shells dropping softly behind.

Gas! GAS! Quick, boys!—An ecstasy of fumbling
Fitting the clumsy helmets just in time;
But someone still was yelling out and stumbling
And flound'ring like a man in fire or lime . . .
Dim through the misty panes and thick green light,
As under a green sea, I saw him drowning.
In all my dreams before my helpless sight,
He plunges at me, guttering, choking, drowning.

If in some smothering dreams, you too could pace
Behind the wagon that we flung him in,
And watch the white eyes writhing in his face,
His hanging face, like a devil's sick of sin;
If you could hear, at every jolt, the blood
Come gargling from the froth-corrupted lungs,
Obscene as cancer, bitter as the cud
Of vile, incurable sores on innocent tongues, —
My friend, you would not tell with such high zest
To children ardent for some desperate glory,
The old Lie: Dulce et decorum est
Pro patria mori.

187

5 November · Remember, Remember · Anon.

In 1605 a group of Catholics plotted to blow up the House of Lords during the State Opening of Parliament. The explosion would have reduced Parliament to a pile of rubble and killed the Protestant King James I. An anonymous letter revealing the plot led to a search of the House of Lords on the night of 4 November – and the discovery of Guy Fawkes guarding 36 barrels of gunpowder! Guy Fawkes and the Gunpowder Plot are now remembered every year on 5 November in the form of extravagant firework displays, and huge bonfires with a straw dummy of Guy traditionally thrown on the top.

Remember, remember the fifth of November
Gunpowder, treason and plot.
I see no reason why gunpowder treason
Should ever be forgot.

Guy Fawkes, Guy, 'twas his intent
To blow up king and parliament.
Three score barrels were laid below
To prove old England's overthrow.

By God's mercy he was catch'd
With a darkened lantern and burning match.
So holler, boys, holler, boys, let the bells ring.
Holler, boys, holler, boys, God save the king!

And what shall we do with him?
Burn him!

5 **November** · Please to Remember ·
Walter de la Mare

In celebration of the King's survival, bonfires were lit around the country. This tradition has only grown over the last few centuries, with the addition of fireworks, and, of course, a Guy atop the bonfire.

> Here am I,
> A poor old Guy:
> Legs in a bonfire,
> Head in the sky;
>
> Shoeless my toes,
> Wild stars behind,
> Smoke in my nose,
> And my eye-peeps blind;
>
> Old hat, old straw –
> In this disgrace;
> While the wildfire gleams
> On a mask for my face.
>
> Ay, all I am made of
> Only trash is:
> And soon – soon,
> Will be dust and ashes.

6 November · *from* Amours de Voyage · Arthur Hugh Clough

Wilfred Owen was not the first poet to interrogate
Horace's phrase 'Dulce et decorum est pro patria mori'.
This extract is taken from Arthur Hugh Clough's mid-
nineteenth-century poem 'Amours de Voyage', set
during the Siege of Rome in 1849. Here, too, Horace's
patriotic phrase is shown to be an idealistic, unrealistic
vision of war.

Dulce it is, and decorum, no doubt, for the country to fall,
    — to
Offer one's blood an oblation to Freedom, and die for the
    Cause; yet
Still, individual culture is also something, and no man
Finds quite distinct the assurance that he of all others is
    called on,
Or would be justified even, in taking away from the world
    that
Precious creature, himself. Nature sent him here to abide
    here;
Else why send him at all? Nature wants him still, it is
    likely;
On the whole, we are meant to look after ourselves; it is
    certain
Each has to eat for himself, digest for himself, and in
    general
Care for his own dear life, and see to his own
    preservation;

Nature's intentions, in most things uncertain, in this are
  decisive;
Which, on the whole, I conjecture the Romans will
  follow, and I shall.
So we cling to our rocks like limpets; Ocean may bluster,
Over and under and round us; we open our shells to
  imbibe our
Nourishment, close them again, and are safe, fulfilling
  the purpose
Nature intended, — a wise one, of course, and a noble, we
  doubt not.
Sweet it may be and decorous, perhaps, for the country to
  die; but,
On the whole, we conclude the Romans won't do it, and I
  sha'n't.

☾ **6 November** · November Night · Adelaide Crapsey

Adelaide Crapsey was the inventor of the lesser-known poetic form called the 'cinquain'. The name refers to the form's five lines, but there are other, extraordinarily compromising features to the form: the lines rise in syllable count from 2, 4, 6, 8, and back to 2 for the final line, and they follow a stress count of 1, 2, 3, 4, and 1 again for the last line. Whether you stop to count syllables and stresses or not, it lends the poem an undeniably pulsating rhythm.

Listen . . .
With faint dry sound,
Like steps of passing ghosts,
The leaves, frost-crisped, break from the trees
And fall.

7 **November** · The Dead · Rupert Brooke

This beautiful sonnet by Rupert Brooke was written shortly after the outbreak of the First World War. War often transforms humans into statistics. Individual lives become just part of a number of people who died in battle. Yet Brooke's poem stresses the unique experience of those who fought in the war – the music they heard, the friends they had, the moments they spent alone. Brooke himself died in 1915 from an insect bite, whilst serving on a British Naval vessel just off the coast of the Greek island of Skyros.

These hearts were woven of human joys and cares,
    Washed marvellously with sorrow, swift to mirth.
The years had given them kindness. Dawn was theirs,
    And sunset, and the colours of the earth.
These had seen movement, and heard music; known
    Slumber and waking; loved; gone proudly friended;
Felt the quick stir of wonder; sat alone;
    Touched flowers and furs and cheeks. All this is ended.

There are waters blown by changing winds to laughter
And lit by the rich skies, all day. And after,
    Frost, with a gesture, stays the waves that dance
And wandering loveliness. He leaves a white
    Unbroken glory, a gathered radiance,
A width, a shining peace, under the night.

193

William Shakespeare

This song is sung at the end of the second act of
Shakespeare's comedy *As You Like It*, when the runaway
gentleman, Orlando, and his old faithful servant, Adam,
arrive at the court of an exiled Duke who is living as an
outlaw in the Forest of Arden. Despite the song's many
references to human ingratitude and feigned friendship,
the travellers receive a hearty welcome at the feast.

Blow, blow, thou winter wind,
  Thou art not so unkind
    As man's ingratitude;
  Thy tooth is not so keen,
Because thou art not seen,
    Although thy breath be rude.
Heigh-ho! sing, heigh-ho! unto the green holly:
Most friendship is feigning, most loving mere folly:
  Then, heigh-ho, the holly!
    This life is most jolly.

Freeze, freeze, thou bitter sky,
That dost not bite so nigh
  As benefits forgot:
Though thou the waters warp,
  Thy sting is not so sharp
  As friend remembered not.
Heigh-ho! sing, heigh-ho! unto the green holly . . .
Most friendship is feigning, most loving mere folly:
  Then, heigh-ho, the holly!
    This life is most jolly.

8 November · The Leader · Roger McGough

Election Day in the United States of America falls on 'the first Tuesday after November 1'; President Donald Trump was elected on this day in 2016.

> I wanna be the leader
> I wanna be the leader
> Can I be the leader?
> Can I? I can?
> Promise? Promise?
> Yippee, I'm the leader
> I'm the leader
>
> OK what shall we do?

Do you have a place you can go when you feel like being on your own? Sometimes we all feel like we need a bit of time to ourselves. 'Solitude' means the state of being alone, and this poem by A. A. Milne describes a place where the speaker can find solitude, and peace and quiet.

> I have a house where I go
>   When there's too many people,
> I have a house where I go
>   Where no one can be;
> I have a house where I go,
> Where nobody ever says 'No'
> Where no one says anything – so
>   There is no one but me.

9 November · Here Dead We Lie · A. E. Housman

Like Wilfred Owen and Rupert Brooke, A. E. Housman wrote some of his most famous poetry during the Great War. This poem reminds us that many of the soldiers were very young.

> Here dead we lie
> Because we did not choose
> To live and shame the land
> From which we sprung.
>
> Life, to be sure,
> Is nothing much to lose,
> But young men think it is,
> And we were young.

9 November · Divali · David Harmer

Divali is India's largest festival, and a national holiday in India, Nepal, Sri Lanka and Singapore. It falls in the Hindu month of Kartik, which is usually sometime in October or November. 'Divali' means 'rows of lighted lamps', and it is a festival of light and joy: people often celebrate by decorating their houses or shops with colourful lights and lamps. The festival worships Lord Ganesh for welfare and prosperity, and the goddess Lakshmi for wealth and wisdom.

Winter stalks us
like a leopard in the mountains
scenting prey.

It grows dark,
bare trees stick black bars
across the moon's silver eye.

I will light my lamp for you
Lakshmi,
drive away the darkness.

Welcome you into my home
Lakshmi,
beckon you from every window

With light that blazes
out like flames
across the somber sky.

Certain houses
crouch in shadow, do not hear
your gentle voice.

Will not feel
your gentle heartbeat
bring prosperity and fortune.

Darkness hunts them
like a leopard in the mountains
stalking prey.

10 November · The African Lion · A. E. Housman

On this day in 1871, the reporter Henry Morton Stanley met with the explorer and missionary David Livingstone in Zanzibar, in modern Tanzania. Livingstone had been out of contact with Britain for six years, and was presumed by many to be dead. During his years in Africa, Livingstone survived an attack from a lion escaping with only a broken arm. This poem by A.E. Housman is about a ferocious and ravenous lion – but the boys here aren't quite as lucky as Livingstone was!

To meet a bad lad on the African waste
  Is a thing that a lion enjoys;
But he rightly and strongly objects to the taste
  Of good and uneatable boys.

When he bites off a piece of a boy of that sort
  He spits it right out of his mouth,
And retires with a loud and dissatisfied snort
  To the east, or the west, or the south.

So lads of good habits, on coming across
  A lion, need feel no alarm
For they know they are sure to escape with the loss
  Of a leg, or a head, or an arm.

☾ 10 November · *from* The Song of Hiawatha · Henry Wadsworth Longfellow

The Song of Hiawatha is an epic poem by Henry Wadsworth Longfellow that was published in America in 1855. The hero of the poem is the Native American Hiawatha, the son of the beautiful Wenonah and the West Wind. The poem was loosely based on Native American legends, although Longfellow was not very faithful to them, and it is largely set on the shore of Lake Superior, which is called Gitchigume by the Ojibwe Native Americans.

By the shores of Gitche Gumee,
By the shining Big-Sea-Water,
Stood the wigwam of Nokomis,
Daughter of the Moon, Nokomis.
Dark behind it rose the forest,
Rose the black and gloomy pine-trees,
Rose the firs with cones upon them;
Bright before it beat the water,
Beat the clear and sunny water,
Beat the shining Big-Sea-Water.
   There the wrinkled old Nokomis
Nursed the little Hiawatha,
Rocked him in his linden cradle.
Bedded soft in moss and rushes,
Safely bound with reindeer sinews;
Stilled his fretful wail by saying,
'Hush! the Naked Bear will hear thee!'
Lulled him into slumber, singing,

'Ewa-yea! my little owlet!
Who is this, that lights the wigwam?
With his great eyes lights the wigwam?
Ewa-yea! my little owlet!'
    Many things Nokomis taught him
Of the stars that shine in heaven;
Showed him Ishkoodah, the comet,
Ishkoodah, with fiery tresses;
Showed the Death-Dance of the spirits,
Warriors with their plumes and war-clubs,
Flaring far away to northward
In the frosty nights of Winter;
Showed the vorad whit road in heaven,
Pathway of the ghosts, the shadows,
Running straight across the heaven,
Crowded with the ghosts, the shadows.

11 November · The Soldier · Rupert Brooke

On 11 November 1918, the fighting ceased on the Western Front, marking the end of World War One. At the eleventh hour of the eleventh day of the eleventh month, people all round the world hold a two-minute silence to mark their respect for the dead. 11 November is known as Armistice or Remembrance Day. This poem was written in 1914, just as the war was about to begin, and is one of the most well-known poems from the war: it is notable for its lack of gruesome imagery, and a seemingly idealistic vision of how noble it is to die for your country.

If I should die, think only this of me:
    That there's some corner of a foreign field
That is for ever England. There shall be
    In that rich earth a richer dust concealed;
A dust whom England bore, shaped, made aware,
    Gave, once, her flowers to love, her ways to roam;
A body of England's, breathing English air,
    Washed by the rivers, blest by suns of home.

And think, this heart, all evil shed away,
    A pulse in the eternal mind, no less
        Gives somewhere back the thoughts by England
            given;
Her sights and sounds; dreams happy as her day;
    And laughter, learnt of friends; and gentleness,
        In hearts at peace, under an English heaven.

11 November · In Flanders Fields · John McCrae

John McCrae was a Canadian doctor who served as a Lieutenant-Colonel in the First World War. The poem was published in 1915, and its immediate success led to it being quoted in propaganda as part of the war efforts. Its reference to the red poppies of Flanders led to the symbolic wearing of poppies on Remembrance Day each year. McCrae died of pneumonia during combat service in 1918, just eight months before the war ended.

In Flanders fields the poppies blow
Between the crosses, row on row,
   That mark our place; and in the sky
   The larks, still bravely singing, fly
Scarce heard amid the guns below.

We are the Dead. Short days ago
We lived, felt dawn, saw sunset glow,
   Loved and were loved, and now we lie
   In Flanders fields.

Take up our quarrel with the foe:
To you from failing hands we throw
   The torch; be yours to hold it high.
   If ye break faith with us who die
We shall not sleep, though poppies grow
   In Flanders fields.

12 November · 'No One Cares Less than I' · Edward Thomas

In this poem Edward Thomas can be seen to parody the opening lines of Brooke's 'The Soldier'. In response to Brooke's notion that, should he die in 'some corner of a foreign field', that place shall be 'for ever England', Thomas responds that he doesn't care whether he is 'destined to lie / Under a foreign clod'. Here the poet warns the reader of the dangers of patriotism and the glorification of war. Thomas died on 9 April 1917 in Pas-de-Calais, France. He was thirty-nine years old.

'No one cares less than I,
Nobody knows but God,
Whether I am destined to lie
Under a foreign clod,'
Were the words I made to the bugle call in the morning.

But laughing, storming, scorning,
Only the bugles know
What the bugles say in the morning,
And they do not care, when they blow
The call that I heard and made words to early this
    morning.

12 November · *from* Epitaphs of the War · Rudyard Kipling

'Epitaphs of the War' is a collection of short poems and fragments. Kipling's eighteen-year-old son John was killed in 1915. In the early months of the conflict, Kipling had been in favour of the British war effort, and he himself had pushed for John to join the army. Yet the bitter phrasing of 'Common Form' here expresses a deeply critical view both of the war and of Kipling's own actions as a father.

Batteries out of Ammunition

If any mourn us in the workshop, say
We died because the shift kept holiday.

Common Form

If any question why we died,
Tell them, because our fathers lied.

A Dead Statesman

I could not dig: I dared not rob:
Therefore I lied to please the mob.
Now all my lies are proved untrue
And I must face the men I slew.
What tale shall serve me here among
Mine angry and defrauded young?

13 November · An Irish Airman Foresees his Death · W. B. Yeats

Yeats wrote this poem in 1918, towards the end of the war. Ireland's involvement in the Great War was greatly complicated. Ireland, which was then part of the United Kingdom, initially offered unanimous support to England in the war; however, advocation of Irish independence from British rule led to the Easter Rising of 1916, when a band of armed activists seized key locations in Dublin and proclaimed Ireland a republic. Yeats's Irish airman captures a sense of this ambivalence; he neither hates his enemy nor loves his allies.

I know that I shall meet my fate
Somewhere among the clouds above;
Those that I fight I do not hate,
Those that I guard I do not love;
My country is Kiltartan Cross,
My countrymen Kiltartan's poor,
No likely end could bring them loss
Or leave them happier than before.
Nor law, nor duty bade me fight,
Nor public man, nor cheering crowds,
A lonely impulse of delight
Drove to this tumult in the clouds;
I balanced all, brought all to mind,
The years to come seemed waste of breath,
A waste of breath the years behind
In balance with this life, this death.

13 November · Does it Matter? ·
Siegfried Sassoon

Siegfried Sassoon joined the British Army shortly before the outbreak of the First World War in 1914. By 1917, many of his friends and comrades had been killed, including his brother, and despite being awarded the Military Cross for several acts of bravery, he was bitterly disillusioned with the war. Many of Sassoon's poems contain a powerful anti-war message, and 'Does it Matter?' is no exception. The bitter sarcasm of the title is carried through the rest of the poem, as he describes men whose lives and bodies have been ruined by war.

Does it matter? – losing your legs?
For people will always be kind,
And you need not show that you mind
When others come in after hunting
To gobble their muffins and eggs.

Does it matter? – losing your sight?
There's such splendid work for the blind;
And people will always be kind,
As you sit on the terrace remembering
And turning your face to the light.

Do they matter from those dreams – the pit?
You can drink and forget and be glad,
And people won't say that you're mad;
For they'll know that you've fought for your country,
And no one will worry a bit.

207

14 November · Anthem for Doomed Youth · Wilfred Owen

This First World War poem takes the surprising form of a sonnet – a form usually associated with love poetry. Among the deadliest of conflicts in human history, World War One saw the deaths of over 17 million people. Owen's poetry marks an attempt to deal with this immense loss of human life – and also an acknowledgement that such loss is beyond comprehension.

What passing-bells for these who die as cattle?
   – Only the monstrous anger of the guns.
   Only the stuttering rifles' rapid rattle
Can patter out their hasty orisons.
No mockeries now for them; no prayers nor bells;
   Nor any voice of mourning save the choirs, –
The shrill, demented choirs of wailing shells;
   And bugles calling for them from sad shires.

What candles may be held to speed them all?
   Not in the hands of boys, but in their eyes
Shall shine the holy glimmers of goodbyes.
   The pallor of girls' brows shall be their pall;
Their flowers the tenderness of patient minds,
And each slow dusk a drawing-down of blinds.

14 November • My First Day at School • Michaela Morgan

On this day in 1960, in New Orleans, Louisiana, a six-year-old girl named Ruby Bridges became the first African-American child to go to a previously all-white elementary school. She was escorted by armed guards who protected her from crowds of angry protesters. When we think back to our own first days at school, and the anxiety that comes from being a new face in any context, it becomes impossible to imagine how Ruby must have felt.

I remember . . .
Momma scrubbed my face, hard.
Plaited my hair, tight.
Perched a hopeful white bow on my head,
Like a butterfly hoping for flight.

She shone my shoes, black, shiny, neat.
Another hopeful bow, on each toe,
To give wings to my feet.

My dress was standing to attention, stiff with starch.
My little battledress.
And now, my march.

Two marshals march in front of me.
Two marshals march behind of me.
The people scream and jeer at me.
Their faces are red, not white.

The marshals tower above me, a grey-legged wall.
Broad of back, white of face and tall, tall, tall.
I only see their legs and shoes, as black and shiny as mine.
They march along, stern and strong. I try to march in
    time.

One hisses to another, 'Slow down it ain't a race.
She only take little bitty girlie steps.'
I quicken my pace.

Head up.
Eyes straight.
I march into school.
To learn like any other kid can.

And maybe to teach a lesson too.

15 November · Sympathy ·
Paul Laurence Dunbar

Paul Laurence Dunbar was an African-American poet, novelist, and playwright in the late nineteenth and early twentieth century. As one of the earliest internationally successful African-American writers, his work has proven to be hugely influential. Maya Angelou cites Dunbar as a major influence, and she took the title for her autobiography, *I Know Why the Caged Bird Sings*, from this poem.

I know what the caged bird feels, alas!
When the sun is bright on the upland slopes;
When the wind stirs soft through the springing grass,
And the river flows like a stream of glass;
When the first bird sings and the first bud opes,
And the faint perfume from its chalice steals –
I know what the caged bird feels!

I know why the caged bird beats his wing
Till its blood is red on the cruel bars;
For he must fly back to his perch and cling
When he fain would be on the bough a-swing;
And a pain still throbs in the old, old scars
And they pulse again with a keener sting –
I know why he beats his wing!

I know why the caged bird sings, ah me,
When his wing is bruised and his bosom sore, —
When he beats his bars and he would be free;
It is not a carol of joy or glee,
But a prayer that he sends from his heart's deep core,
But a plea, that upward to Heaven he flings —
I know why the caged bird sings!

15 November · Fiere Good Nicht · Jackie Kay (after Gussie Lord Davis)

This poem is taken from the award-winning Scottish Makar Jackie Kay's 2011 collection, *Fiere*, and it's a perfect poem to read just before going to bed. In the Scots dialect, 'fiere' means 'mate' or 'companion' – and this is just one of the many Scots terms used in the poem.

When you've had your last one for the road,
a Linkwood, a Talisker, a Macallan,
and you've finished your short story
and played one more time Nacht und Traume
with Roland Hayes singing sweetly;
and pictured yourself on the road,
the one that stretches to infinity,
and said good night to your dead,
and fathomed the links in the long day –
then it's time to say Goodnight fiere,
and lay your highland head on your feather pillow,
far away – in England, Canada, New Zealand –
and coorie in, coorie in, coorie in.
The good dreams are drifting quietly doon,
like a figmaleerie, my fiere, my dearie,
and you'll sleep as soond as a peerie,
and you, are turning slowly towards the licht:
Goodnight fiere, fiere, Good Nicht.

16 November · On the Vanity of Earthly Greatness · Arthur Guiterman

The beloved American humourist Arthur Guiterman seems to have been inspired by Polonius's maxim from Hamlet about brevity being the soul of wit. Light-hearted, but often containing touches of darkness, Guiterman's punchy rhyming verses sharply skewer the absurdities of all facets of life – and death. Here he uses bathos to wonderful effect as he amusingly contrasts the former greatness of beasts and rulers with their rather more modest afterlives.

The tusks which clashed in mighty brawls
Of mastodons, are billiard balls.

The sword of Charlemagne the Just
Is ferric oxide, known as rust.

The grizzly bear, whose potent hug,
Was feared by all, is now a rug.

Great Caesar's bust is on the shelf,
And I don't feel so well myself.

16 November · The Wind and the Moon · George MacDonald

On mid-November nights, the wind can blow bitterly and moonlight can make the frost-covered earth shimmer and sparkle. This fantastic poem by George MacDonald imagines both the wind and the moon as people, supplying them with personalities and feelings. The poem has a strange visual shape, juxtaposing very short and rather long lines in a way which imitates the gusts of wind, blowing fiercely for a moment before subsiding. With its quick-fire rhymes and humorous twist, this is a great poem to read aloud.

Said the Wind to the Moon, 'I will blow you out;
You stare
In the air
Like a ghost in a chair,
Always looking what I am about –
I hate to be watched; I'll blow you out.'

The Wind blew hard, and out went the Moon.
So deep
On a heap
Of clouds to sleep,
Down lay the Wind, and slumbered soon,
Muttering low, 'I've done for that Moon.'

He turned in his bed; she was there again!
On high
In the sky,
With her one ghost eye,
The Moon shone white and alive and plain.
Said the Wind, 'I will blow you out again.'

The Wind blew hard, and the Moon grew slim.
'With my sledge
And my wedge,
I have knocked off her edge!
If only I blow right fierce and grim,
The creature will soon be slimmer than slim.'

He blew and he blew, and she thinned to a thread.
'One puff
More's enough
To blow her to snuff!
One good puff more where the last was bred,
And glimmer, glimmer, glum will go the thread.'

He blew a great blast, and the thread was gone.
In the air
Nowhere
Was a moonbeam bare;
Far off and harmless the shy stars shone –
Sure and certain the Moon was gone!

The Wind he took to his revels once more;
On down
In town,
Like a merry-mad clown.
He leaped and hallooed with whistle and roar –
'What's that?' The glimmering thread once more!

He flew in a rage – he danced and blew;
But in vain
Was the pain
Of his bursting brain;
For still the broader the Moon-scrap grew,
The broader he swelled his big cheeks and blew.

Slowly she grew – till she filled the night,
And shone
On her throne
In the sky alone,
A matchless, wonderful silvery light,
Radiant and lovely, the queen of the night.

Said the Wind: 'What a marvel of power am I!
With my breath,
In good faith
I blew her to death!
First blew her away right out of the sky –
Then blew her in; what strength have I!'

But the Moon she knew nothing about the affair;
For high
In the sky,
With her one white eye,
Motionless, miles above the air,
She had never heard the great Wind blare.

17 November · The Duke of Fire and the Duchess of Ice · Carol Ann Duffy

We all know the phrase 'Opposites attract', but can you imagine how difficult life would be if spending time with your opposite meant turning into a puddle? Like the previous poem, this piece by the former Poet Laureate Carol Ann Duffy is about an unlikely couple – a duke made of fire and a duchess of ice.

Passionate love for the Duke of Fire
the Duchess of Ice felt.
One kiss was her heart's desire,
but with one kiss she would melt.

She dreamed of him in his red pantaloons,
in his orange satin blouse,
in his crimson cravat,
in his tangerine hat,
in his vermilion dancing shoes.

One kiss, one kiss,
lips of flame on frost,
one kiss, pure bliss,
and never count the cost.

She woke. She went to the bathroom.
She took a freezing shower –
her body as pale as a stalagmite,
winter's frailest flower.

The Duke of Fire stood there,
radiant, ablaze with love,
and the Duchess of Ice cared nothing
for anything in the world.

She spoke his name,
her voice was snow,
kissed him, kissed him again,
and in his warm, passionate arms
turned to water, tears, rain.

17 November · Written with a Diamond on her Window at Woodstock · Elizabeth I

Elizabeth I was crowned on 17 November 1558. Before
Elizabeth's own reign, she was accused of conspiring
against her sister, Mary I. Elizabeth was imprisoned
in the Tower of London, and, after two months, she
was moved to Woodstock, in Oxfordshire, where she
was kept under the equivalent of house arrest. There
she was said to have carved the following words into a
windowpane, using the sharp point of a diamond. The
lines were published in 1563 by the historian John Foxe.

> Much suspected by me,
> Nothing proved can be,
> Quoth Elizabeth prisoner.

18 November • Overheard on a Saltmarsh • Harold Munro

This imagined conversation is an especially good poem for two people to read aloud, with one person taking the role of the jealous goblin, and the other acting out the part of the beautiful nymph.

Nymph, nymph, what are your beads?

Green glass, goblin. Why do you stare at them?

Give them me.

       No.

Give them me. Give them me.

            No.

Then I will howl all night in the reeds,
lie in the mud and howl for them.

Goblin, why do you love them so?

They are better than stars or water,
Better than voices of winds that sing,
Better than any man's fair daughter,
Your green glass beads on a silver ring.

Hush, I stole them out of the moon.

Give me your beads, I want them.

            No.

I will howl in a deep lagoon
For your green glass beads, I love them so.
Give them me. Give them.

       No.

18 November · Tell as a Marksman – were forgotten · Emily Dickinson

On 18 November 1307, William Tell is said to have shot an arrow through an apple on top of his son's head. Tell is a figure of legend, much like Robin Hood, and is considered a liberation hero who refused to bow to the brutal Habsburg bailiff Gessler. The American poet Emily Dickinson takes this legendary tale of Tell as the subject of her powerful poem.

Tell as a Marksman – were forgotten
Tell – this Day endures
Ruddy as that coeval Apple
The Tradition bears –

Fresh as Mankind that humble story
Though a statelier Tale
Grown in the Repetition hoary
Scarcely would prevail –

Tell had a son – The ones that knew it
Need not linger here –
Those who did not to Human Nature
Will subscribe a Tear –

Tell would not bare his Head
In Presence
Of the Ducal Hat –
Threatened for that with Death – by Gessler –
Tyranny bethought

Make of his only Boy a Target
That surpasses Death –
Stolid to Love's supreme entreaty
Not forsook of Faith –

Mercy of the Almighty begging –
Tell his Arrow sent –
God it is said replies in Person
When the cry is meant –

19 November · The Gettysburg Address · Abraham Lincoln

On 19 November 1863, President Abraham Lincoln delivered the Gettysburg Address at the Consecration ceremony of the National Cemetery at Gettysburg, on the site of one of the climactic battles of the American Civil War. In just over two minutes, Lincoln brilliantly stated that the war efforts were not in vain, but were aimed towards the great cause of human equality.

Four score and seven years ago our fathers brought forth on this continent, a new nation, conceived in Liberty, and dedicated to the proposition that all men are created equal.

Now we are engaged in a great civil war, testing whether that nation, or any nation so conceived and so dedicated, can long endure. We are met on a great battlefield of that war. We have come to dedicate a portion of that field, as a final resting place for those who here gave their lives that that nation might live. It is altogether fitting and proper that we should do this.

But, in a larger sense, we can not dedicate – we can not consecrate – we can not hallow – this ground. The brave men, living and dead, who struggled here, have consecrated it, far above our poor power to add or detract. The world will little note, nor long remember what we say here, but it can never forget what they did here. It is for us the living, rather, to be dedicated here to the unfinished work which they who fought here have thus far so nobly advanced. It is rather for us to be here, dedicated to the great task remaining before us – that from these honored dead we take increased devotion to that cause for which they gave the last full measure of devotion – that we here highly resolve that these dead shall not have died in vain – that this nation, under God, shall have a new birth of freedom – and that government of the people, by the people, for the people, shall not perish from the earth.

19 November · Abraham Lincoln · Abraham Lincoln

Lincoln was not necessarily a born orator. The following squib was found in the margin of his childhood maths book.

Abraham Lincoln
his hand and pen
he will be good but
god knows When

20 November · *from* The Prophet ·
Kahlil Gibran

20 November is Children's Day: a day that celebrates
children's education, health, rights and well-being
around the world. Kahlil Gibran was a Lebanese-
American poet and artist. This poem offers the powerful
image of children as 'living arrows' sent forth.

Your children are not your children.
They are the sons and daughters of Life's longing for
    itself.
They come through you but not from you,
And though they are with you yet they belong not to you.

You may give them your love but not your thoughts,
For they have their own thoughts.
You may house their bodies but not their souls,
For their souls dwell in the house of tomorrow,
which you cannot visit, not even in your dreams.
You may strive to be like them,
but seek not to make them like you.
For life goes not backward nor tarries with yesterday.

You are the bows from which your children
as living arrows are sent forth.
The archer sees the mark upon the path of the infinite,
and He bends you with His might
that His arrows may go swift and far.
Let your bending in the archer's hand be for gladness;
For even as He loves the arrow that flies,
so He loves also the bow that is stable.

☾ 20 November· The Moon was but a Chin of Gold • Emily Dickinson

In this poem, Emily Dickinson marvels at the changes that happen to the moon every month: the narrator of the poem seems surprised that the moon can evolve so quickly from a thin 'Chin of Gold' to a full, 'perfect Face' just over the course of 'a Night or two'.

The Moon was but a Chin of Gold
A Night or two ago—
And now she turns Her perfect Face
Upon the World below—

Her Forehead is of Amplest Blonde—
Her Cheek—a Beryl hewn—
Her Eye unto the Summer Dew
The likest I have known—

Her Lips of Amber never part—
But what must be the smile
Upon Her Friend she could confer
Were such Her Silver Will—

And what a privilege to be
But the remotest Star—
For Certainty She take Her Way
Beside Your Palace Door—

Her Bonnet is the Firmament—
The Universe—Her Shoe—
The Stars—the Trinkets at Her Belt—
Her Dimities—of Blue—

21 November · Autumn · John Clare

In these evocative, almost painterly lines, John
Clare transports us to an autumnal pastoral scene by
appealing to a combination of senses. We can feel the
residual heat of summer, hear the restless activity of
birds and see the rich, saturated colours of a landscape
in transition from verdant greens to more fiery hues. To
take all of this in at once, Clare suggests, is to appreciate
not just a single fleeting moment, but to experience
nature as something altogether more timeless and
transcendent.

The thistledown's flying, though the winds are all still,
On the green grass now lying, now mounting the hill,
The spring from the fountain now boils like a pot;
Through stones past the counting it bubbles red-hot.

The ground parched and cracked is like overbaked bread,
The greensward all wracked is, bents dried up and dead.
The fallow fields glitter like water indeed,
And gossamers twitter, flung from weed unto weed.

Hill-tops like hot iron glitter bright in the sun,
And the rivers we're eying burn to gold as they run;
Burning hot is the ground, liquid gold is the air;
Whoever looks round sees Eternity there.

In this remarkably pithy poem the American writer Amy Lowell manages to distill the very essence of an autumn evening. Here she captures the unceasing changeability of the season and the otherworldliness of nights caught between the brightness of summer and total darkness of winter. It is freighted by a certain bittersweetness, as there's an implicit solitude to the narrator having spent a day idly staring at leaves, but the poem ultimately ends on a hopeful note with Lowell redefining autumn as a season not of decay, but ethereal beauty. All that in just four lines.

> All day I have watched the purple vine leaves
> Fall into the water.
> And now in the moonlight they still fall,
> But each leaf is fringed with silver.

22 November · A Word is Dead · Emily Dickinson

Emily Dickinson wrote many brief poems, but this
is one of her shortest works. Although some people
believe that words 'die' once they are spoken, Dickinson
is suggesting that they begin to take on a whole new life
once they have been said.

> A word is dead
> When it is said,
> Some say.
> I say it just
> Begins to live
> That day.

22 November · The Runaway · Robert Frost

A 'Morgan' is a small and sturdy type of horse bred in
New England. The colt in this poem has never seen
snow before. He runs around his pasture panicking:
he doesn't understand the cold, wet prickles all over
his coat, and white dots swirling around, obscuring his
vision.

Once when the snow of the year was beginning to fall,
We stopped by a mountain pasture to say, 'Whose colt?'
A little Morgan had one forefoot on the wall,
The other curled at his breast. He dipped his head
And snorted to us. And then we saw him bolt.
We heard the miniature thunder where he fled,
And we saw him, or thought we saw him, dim and gray,
Like a shadow across instead of behind the flakes.
The little fellow's afraid of the falling snow.
He never saw it before. It isn't play
With the little fellow at all. He's running away.
He wouldn't believe when his mother told him, 'Sakes,
It's only weather.' He thought she didn't know!
So this is something he has to bear alone
And now he comes again with a clatter of stone,
He mounts the wall again with whited eyes
Dilated nostrils, and tail held straight up straight.
He shudders his coat as if to throw off flies.
'Whoever it is that leaves him out so late,
When all other creatures have gone to stall and bin,
Ought to be told to come and take him in.'

231

23 November · Not Waving but Drowning · Stevie Smith

This poem by Stevie Smith was published in 1957. In an interview about the poem, Smith said that it was about how many people pretend out of bravery that they are 'very jolly and ordinary sort of chaps', when, actually, they find life to be a real struggle – they're not waving, but drowning.

Nobody heard him, the dead man,
But still he lay moaning:
I was much further out than you thought
And not waving but drowning.

Poor chap, he always loved larking
And now he's dead
It must have been too cold for him his heart gave way,
They said.

Oh, no no no, it was too cold always
(Still the dead one lay moaning)
I was much too far out all my life
And not waving but drowning.

23 November · Funeral Blues · W. H. Auden

'Funeral Blues' was read out in its entirety in the romantic comedy *Four Weddings and a Funeral*, and has become one of Auden's best-known poems. 'Funeral Blues' details the grief of the speaker for their lover, moving from imagery of the couple's shared domestic life – clocks and telephones – to demanding that the whole nation join in the mourning, even the traffic policemen and the 'public doves'.

Stop all the clocks, cut off the telephone,
Prevent the dog from barking with a juicy bone,
Silence the pianos and with muffled drum
Bring out the coffin, let the mourners come.

Let aeroplanes circle moaning overhead
Scribbling on the sky the message, He is dead.
Put crepe bows round the white necks of the public doves,
Let the traffic policemen wear black cotton gloves.

He was my North, my South, my East and West,
My working week and my Sunday rest,
My noon, my midnight, my talk, my song;
I thought that love would last for ever: I was wrong.

The stars are not wanted now: put out every one;
Pack up the moon and dismantle the sun;
Pour away the ocean and sweep up the wood.
For nothing now can ever come to any good.

☀ **24 November** • Prayer for Earth •
Myra Cohn Livingston

Throughout much of the world, nature is under threat —
forests are being cut down, rivers polluted, and animals
dying. This short poem vividly captures two beautiful
moments in nature, and offers a prayer: let this stay.

Last night
an owl
called from the hill.
Coyotes howled.
A deer stood still
nibbling at bushes far away.
The moon shone silver.
Let this stay.

Today
two noisy crows
flew by,
their shadows pasted on the sky.
The sun broke out
through clouds of grey.
An iris opened.
Let this stay.

24 November · Winter Poem ·
Nikki Giovanni

Nikki Giovanni is one of the most celebrated living
African-American poets, and is particularly well known
for her powerful political poetry. This little poem,
however, takes as its subject Winter weather. The poet
brings the wintry setting of the poem to life, giving
snowflakes the ability to feel happy. While the poem
acknowledges that the beautiful snow cannot last
forever, the final image is of new life springing up after
the freezing Winter weather has departed.

once a snowflake fell
on my brow and i loved
it so much and i kissed
it and it was happy and called its cousins
and brothers and a web
of snow engulfed me then
i reached to love them all
and i squeezed them and they became
a spring rain and i stood perfectly
still and was a flower

235

25 November · The New-England Boy's Song about Thanksgiving Day · Lydia Maria Child

Thanksgiving is a holiday that remembers and gives thanks for the kindness that the first pilgrims to America were shown by the Native Americans from the Wampanoag tribe. In 1863, Abraham Lincoln set aside the last Thursday in November as an official national day of Thanksgiving. Nowadays, the holiday is usually celebrated by families and friends enjoying a meal together, often with turkey as the main dish. This poem, by Lydia Maria Child, draws on childhood memories of visits to her grandfather's house.

Over the river, and through the wood,
  To Grandfather's house we go;
    The horse knows the way,
    To carry the sleigh,
  Through the white and drifted snow.

Over the river, and through the wood,
  To Grandfather's house away!
    We would not stop
    For doll or top,
  For 'tis Thanksgiving day.

Over the river, and through the wood,
  Oh, how the wind does blow!
    It stings the toes,
    And bites the nose,
  As over the ground we go.

Over the river, and through the wood,
 With a clear blue winter sky,
  The dogs do bark,
  And children hark,
 As we go jingling by.

Over the river, and through the wood,
 To have a first-rate play —
  Hear the bells ring
  Ting-a-ling-ding,
 Hurra for Thanksgiving day!

Over the river, and through the wood —
 No matter for winds that blow;
  Or if we get
  The sleigh upset,
 Into a bank of snow.

Over the river, and through the wood,
 To see little John and Ann;
  We will kiss them all,
  And play snow-ball,
 And stay as long as we can.

Over the river, and through the wood,
 Trot fast, my dapple grey!
  Spring over the ground,
  Like a hunting hound,
 For 'tis Thanksgiving day!

Over the river, and through the wood,
And straight through the barn-yard gate;
We seem to go
Extremely slow,
It is so hard to wait.

Over the river, and through the wood,
Old Jowler hears our bells;
He shakes his pow,
With a loud bow-wow,
And thus the news he tells.

Over the river, and through the wood –
When Grandmother sees us come,
She will say, Oh dear,
The children are here,
Bring a pie for every one.

Over the river, and through the wood –
Now Grandmother's cap I spy!
Hurra for the fun!
Is the pudding done?
Hurra for the pumpkin pie!

25 November · Benediction · James Berry

This next short poem – or prayer – of thanks is penned by the Jamaican-born British poet James Berry. His acclaimed writings speak often both of his love of Jamaica and his anger at the injustice his forebears suffered at the hands of the colonialists. In this poem, the last two lines focus on unity.

> Thanks to the ear
> that someone may hear
>
> Thanks for seeing
> that someone may see
>
> Thanks for feeling
> that someone may feel
>
> Thanks for touch
> that someone may be touched
>
> Thanks to flowering of white moon
> and spreading shawl of black night
> holding villages and cities together

239

26 November · Signs of the Times · Paul Laurence Dunbar

The fourth Thursday in November marks Thanksgiving Day in the USA. It has been a federal holiday in the States since the Civil War, when President Lincoln proclaimed a day of 'Thanksgiving and Praise to our beneficent Father who dwelleth in the Heavens'. The day is celebrated with televised parades and sports matches, family dinners with turkeys, and the presidential pardoning of one lucky turkey. This poem by Paul Laurence Dunbar, written in southern slang, is a tribute to the day.

Air a-gittin' cool an' coolah,
   Frost a-comin' in de night,
Hicka' nuts an' wa'nuts fallin',
   Possum keepin' out o' sight.
Tu'key struttin' in de ba'nya'd,
   Nary step so proud ez his;
Keep on struttin', Mistah Tu'key,
   Yo' do' know whut time it is.

Cidah press commence a-squeakin'
   Eatin' apples sto'ed away,
Chillun swa'min' 'roun' lak ho'nets,
   Huntin' aigs ermung de hay.
Mistah Tu'key keep on gobblin'
   At de geese a-flyin' souf,
Oomph! dat bird do' know whut's comin';
   Ef he did he'd shet his mouf.

240

Pumpkin gittin' good an' yallah
  Mek me open up my eyes;
Seems lak it's a-lookin' at me
  Jes' a-la'in' dah sayin' 'Pies.'
Tu'key gobbler gwine 'roun' blowin',
  Gwine 'roun' gibbin' sass an' slack;
Keep on talkin', Mistah Tu'key,
  You ain't seed no almanac.

Fa'mer walkin' th'oo de ba'nya'd
  Seein' how things is comin' on,
Sees ef all de fowls is fatt'nin' –
  Good times comin' sho's you bo'n.
Hyeahs dat tu'key gobbler braggin',
  Den his face break in a smile –
Nebbah min', you sassy rascal,
  He's gwine nab you atter while.

Choppin' suet in de kitchen,
  Stonin' raisins in de hall,
Beef a-cookin' fu' de mince meat,
  Spices groun' – I smell 'em all.
Look hyeah, Tu'key, stop dat gobblin',
  You ain' luned de sense ob feah,
You ol' fool, yo' naik's in dangah,
  Do' you know Thanksgibbin's hyeah?

241

☾ 26 November · Immigrant · Fleur Adcock

Fleur Adcock is a poet from New Zealand, who has lived much of her life in the UK. This short poem is about how we identify with a place. It's worth noting that Adcock doesn't tell us which accent she is putting to the test – her old New Zealand one or her new British one?

November '63: eight months in London.
I pause on the low bridge to watch the pelicans:
they float swanlike, arching their white necks
over only slightly ruffled bundles of wings,
burying awkward beaks in the lake's water

I clench cold fists in my Marks and Spencer's jacket
and secretly test my accent once again:
St James's Park, St James's Park, St James's Park.

27 November • Nuns Fret Not at their Convent's Narrow Room • William Wordsworth

Wordsworth was renowned for long blank verse poetry – the use of hundreds of lines of unrhymed iambic pentameter. In a sense, blank verse paved the way for modern free-verse – structureless, rhymeless modern poetry without metre. Wordsworth, however, was a great believer that composing against the constraints of poetry helps us to grapple with our thoughts. While the sonnet form might seem a prison at first glance, Wordsworth compares it to other contained spaces which produce things of beauty – such as nectar from foxglove bells or a wonderful carpet from a loom.

Nuns fret not at their Convent's narrow room;
And Hermits are contented with their Cells;
And Students with their pensive Citadels:
Maids at the Wheel, the Weaver at his Loom,
Sit blithe and happy; Bees that soar for bloom,
High as the highest Peak of Furness Fells,
Will murmur by the hour in Foxglove bells:
In truth the prison, into which we doom
Ourselves, no prison is: and hence to me,
In sundry moods, 'twas pastime to be bound
Within the Sonnet's scanty plot of ground;
Pleased if some Souls (for such there needs must be)
Who have felt the weight of too much liberty,
Should find brief solace there, as I have found.

Although 'Do not go gentle' is commonly thought to have been written about Thomas's dying father, it was actually composed in 1947, five years before his father died. The poet here rails against death and tells us to put up a fight.

Do not go gentle into that good night,
Old age should burn and rave at close of day;
Rage, rage against the dying of the light.

Though wise men at their end know dark is right,
Because their words had forked no lightning they
Do not go gentle into that good night.

Good men, the last wave by, crying how bright
Their frail deeds might have danced in a green bay,
Rage, rage against the dying of the light.

Wild men who caught and sang the sun in flight,
And learn, too late, they grieved it on its way,
Do not go gentle into that good night.

Grave men, near death, who see with blinding sight
Blind eyes could blaze like meteors and be gay,
Rage, rage against the dying of the light.

And you, my father, there on the sad height,
Curse, bless, me now with your fierce tears, I pray.
Do not go gentle into that good night.
Rage, rage against the dying of the light.

28 November · Sonnet 116 ·
William Shakespeare

This is the date in 1582 when, it is thought, William Shakespeare married Anne Hathaway. Sonnet 116, among Shakespeare's most well-known, is about a marriage of minds, and is commonly read at weddings today.

Let me not to the marriage of true minds
Admit impediments; love is not love
Which alters when it alteration finds,
Or bends with the remover to remove.
O no! it is an ever-fixèd mark
That looks on tempests and is never shaken;
It is the star to every wand'ring bark,
Whose worth's unknown, although his height be taken.
Love's not Time's fool, though rosy lips and cheeks
Within his bending sickle's compass come;
Love alters not with his brief hours and weeks,
But bears it out even to the edge of doom.
    If this be error and upon me prov'd,
    I never writ, nor no man ever lov'd.

☾ **28 November** · *from* The Highwayman · Alfred Noyes

First published in 1906, 'The Highwayman' is an evocative narrative poem relating the tragic tale of a highwayman and his lover Bess.

The wind was a torrent of darkness among the gusty trees.
The moon was a ghostly galleon tossed upon cloudy seas.
The road was a ribbon of moonlight over the purple moor,
And the highwayman came riding—
    Riding—riding—
The highwayman came riding, up to the old inn-door.

He'd a French cocked-hat on his forehead, a bunch of
    lace at his chin,
A coat of the claret velvet, and breeches of brown doe-skin.
They fitted with never a wrinkle. His boots were up to
    the thigh.
And he rode with a jewelled twinkle,
    His pistol butts a-twinkle,
His rapier hilt a-twinkle, under the jewelled sky.

Over the cobbles he clattered and clashed in the dark
    inn-yard.
He tapped with his whip on the shutters, but all was
    locked and barred.
He whistled a tune to the window, and who should be
    waiting there
But the landlord's black-eyed daughter,
    Bess, the landlord's daughter,
Plaiting a dark red love-knot into her long black hair.

And dark in the dark old inn-yard a stable-wicket creaked
Where Tim the ostler listened. His face was white and
  peaked.
His eyes were hollows of madness, his hair like mouldy
  hay,
But he loved the landlord's daughter,
    The landlord's red-lipped daughter.
Dumb as a dog he listened, and he heard the robber say—

'One kiss, my bonny sweetheart, I'm after a prize to-night,
But I shall be back with the yellow gold before the
  morning light;
Yet, if they press me sharply, and harry me through the
  day,
Then look for me by moonlight,
    Watch for me by moonlight,
I'll come to thee by moonlight, though hell should bar
  the way.'

He rose upright in the stirrups. He scarce could reach
  her hand,
But she loosened her hair in the casement. His face
  burnt like a brand
As the black cascade of perfume came tumbling over his
  breast;
And he kissed its waves in the moonlight
    (O, sweet black waves in the moonlight!),
Then he tugged at his rein in the moonlight, and
  galloped away to the west.

247

At this time of year the football season is in full swing, and it continues through the winter and spring – which you'll know, of course, if you're as football obsessed as the speaker of this poem!

Five o'clock of a Saturday night,
November out of doors,
We sit down to tea,
My family and me,
To hear the football scores.

I'm the one in our family who tries to listen but everyone else just talks and talks and talks.

Dad discusses his rose trees,
Stephen chokes on his bread,
Grandad moans
About the cold in his bones
And talks about who're dead.

Betty dreams about Terry,
'Who's handsome and ever so tall.'
When Mum joins in
There's such a din
You can't hear the scores at all.

Well a few, but the worst is only hearing half a result, that's very frustrating that is.

Did Fulham win at Fratton Park?
Did Millwall lose at the Den?
What happened to Blackpool at Boothferry Park?
Did Doncaster draw again?

Who dropped a point at Derby?
A fight in crowd at where?
'There's a terrible draught,
I'm freezing to death
And nobody seems to care.'

Who was sent off at Southampton?
Who was booked at West Ham?
'I'm pleased with that rose.'
'Stop picking your nose.'
'Will somebody pass me the jam.'

The Owls beat the Blades in a derby,
Cardiff beat Carlisle three-nil.
'He looks ever so young
With his hair all long.'
'Will someone fetch Grandad his pill.'

Someone lost at the Valley,
The Orient somehow got four.
'You're not to eat jam
With your fingers young man,
You get the knife from the drawer.'

Plymouth Argyle whipped Walsall,
Darlington managed a draw.
'Our Betty, stop dreamin'
And look after Stephen,
He's pouring the sauce on the floor.'

Wrexham romped home at The Racecourse,
The Sandgrounders' winger got three.
'With a touch of compost
And some luck with the frost
We might get some blooms on that tree.'

I've missed Albion and City and Chelsea,
Queens Park and Chester and Crewe.
'Get your grandad his scarf,
There's no need to laugh
We don't want him dying of flu.'

A sudden reversal at Reading,
A last minute winner at York.
'Turn down that radio!
D'you hear what I say to you
I can hardly hear myself talk.'

Yes, but you wait till she wants to listen to something,
I'm not even allowed to breathe. Just to be awkward
everybody goes quiet when the Scottish results come on.

Those strange-sounding teams up in Scotland,
Kilmarnock and Brechin and Clyde,
And players with names like Macintosh,
MacDonald, McNab and Macbride.

Who wants to know about Berwick
Or Forfar, Stranraer and Dundee,
That Hibernian were humbled and Hampden,
That Stirling slammed Celtic eight-three?

The only thing left to do is to go and get the paper.
Trouble is I haven't any money left.

Mum starts clearing the table,
Stacking the plates in the sink.
Would Dad think it funny
If I borrow some money
To buy the *Sporting Pink*?

While Mum's out of the room he slips me five pence.
I'll have to pay him back of course. He's very strict about
things like that, my dad.

I race through the fog up to Jackson's,
Pumping out breath like steam.
I've got to find out
How United made out
They're my favourite team.

So I run my finger down the list of scores looking for the
    result.

United, United, United.
Never mind about the rest.
They've won, they've won,
Like they ought to have done,
Through a last minute header from Best.

When your team wins everything's all right.

I shuffle through leaves in the gutter,
Whistle a tune through my teeth,
Tightrope on walls,
Head imaginary balls,
My family's not bad underneath.

251

☾ 29 November · When You Are Old · W. B. Yeats

Yeats wrote this poem for Maud Gonne, a frequent muse of his, and he emphasizes his belief that, although many have loved her for her youth and beauty, he will be constant in his admiration even when she is 'old and grey'.

When you are old and grey and full of sleep,
And nodding by the fire, take down this book,
And slowly read, and dream of the soft look
Your eyes had once, and of their shadows deep;

How many loved your moments of glad grace,
And loved your beauty with love false or true,
But one man loved the pilgrim soul in you,
And loved the sorrows of your changing face;

And bending down beside the glowing bars,
Murmur, a little sadly, how Love fled
And paced upon the mountains overhead
And hid his face amid a crowd of stars.

30 November · Sing me a Song of a Lad that is Gone · Robert Louis Stevenson

30 November is the feast day of Saint Andrew and is celebrated as a national holiday in Scotland.

Sing me a song of a lad that is gone,
Say, could that lad be I?
Merry of soul he sailed on a day
Over the sea to Skye.

Mull was astern, Rum on the port,
Eigg on the starboard bow;
Glory of youth glowed in his soul;
Where is that glory now?

Sing me a song of a lad that is gone,
Say, could that lad be I?
Merry of soul he sailed on a day
Over the sea to Skye.

Give me again all that was there,
Give me the sun that shone!
Give me the eyes, give me the soul,
Give me the lad that's gone!

Sing me a song of a lad that is gone,
Say, could that lad be I?
Merry of soul he sailed on a day
Over the sea to Skye.

Billow and breeze, islands and seas,
Mountains of rain and sun,
All that was good, all that was fair,
All that was me is gone.

30 November · Nothing Gold Can Stay · Robert Frost

Here the colours of nature fade as Winter approaches, and nothing can stop the passing of time.

> Nature's first green is gold,
> Her hardest hue to hold.
> Her early leaf's a flower;
> But only so an hour.
> Then leaf subsides to leaf.
> So Eden sank to grief,
> So dawn goes down to day.
> Nothing gold can stay.

Index of First Lines

257

Index of Poets and Translators

263

Acknowledgements

The compiler and publisher would like to thank the following for permission to use copyright material:

Adcock, Fleur: 'Immigrant' from *Poems 1960–2000* (Bloodaxe Books, 2000). Copyright © Fleur Adcock. Reproduced with permission of Bloodaxe Books; **Agard, John:** 'The Hurt Boy and the Birds' from *Get Back Pimple* (Penguin, 1997). Copyright © John Agard. All poems published by permission of John Agard c/o the Caroline Sheldon Literary Agency; **Agbabi, Patience:** 'Prologue' from *Transformatrix* (Canongate Books, 2000). Copyright © Patience Agbabi. Reprinted with the permission of Canongate Books Ltd; **Ahlberg, Allan:** 'Please Mrs Butler' and 'Talk us Through it, Charlotte' from *Collected Poems* (Puffin, 2008) copyright © Allan Ahlberg. Reprinted by permission of Penguin Random House; **Armitage, Simon:** 'The Convergence of the Twain' by Simon Armitage and 'Give' from *Paper Aeroplane* by Simon Armitage (Faber & Faber, 2015) copyright © Simon Armitage. Reproduced by permission of Faber & Faber Ltd and by permission of the author; **Auden, W. H.:** 'But I Can't' and 'Funeral Blues' from *Collected Auden* (Faber & Faber, 2004) copyright © W. H. Auden. Reprinted by permission of Curtis Brown Ltd; **Berry, James:** 'Benediction' from *The Story I Am In: Selected Poems* (Bloodaxe Books, 2011). Copyright © James Berry. Reproduced with permission of Bloodaxe Books; **Betjeman, John:** 'Slough' and Diary of a Church Mouse from Collected Poems by John Betjeman. Copyright © The Estate of John Betjeman 1955, 1958, 1960, 1962, 1964, 1966, 1970, 1979, 1981, 1982, 2001. Reproduced by permission of the Estate of John Betjeman; **Burton, Tim**: 'The Girl with Many Eyes', reproduced by permission of the author; **Carter, James:** 'Take a Poem' by James Carter. By permission of the publisher, Otterbarry Books, on behalf of the author; **Clarke, Gillian:** 'Plums' from *Selected Poems* by Gillian Clarke. Published by Carcanet Press, 1996. Copyright © Gillian Clarke. Reproduced by permission of the author c/o Rogers, Coleridge & White Ltd, 20 Powis Mews, London, W11 1JN; **Colum, Padraic:** 'An Old Woman of the Roads' reprinted by permission of The Estate of Padraic Colum; **Cope, Wendy,** 'An Attempt at Unrhymed Verse' from *Two Cures for Love* (Faber & Faber, 2009) copyright © Wendy Cope 2008. Reproduced by permission of Faber & Faber Ltd; **Crossan, Sarah:** 'Hornbeacon High' an excerpt taken from *One* (Bloomsbury, 2015) copyright © Sarah Crossan. Used with permission of Bloomsbury Publishing Plc; **Cummings, E. E.:** 'l(a' copyright © 1958, 1986, 1991 by Trustees for the E. E. Cummings Trust. Used by permission of Liveright Publishing Corporation;

267

Dahl, Roald: 'Television' from *Charlie and the Chocolate Factory* (Penguin, 1964) and 'Down Vith Children!' from *The Witches* (Jonathan Cape & Penguin Books, 1983). Copyright © Roald Dahl. All poems published by permission of David Higham Associates on behalf of the estate of the author; **de la Mare, Walter:** 'Please to Remember' and 'Someone' by permission of The Literary Trustees of Walter de la Mare and the Society of Authors as their representative; **Dharker, Imtiaz:** 'The Right Word' from *The Terrorist at my table* (Bloodaxe Books, 2006) and 'Crab-Apples' from *I Speak for the Devil* (Bloodaxe Books, 2001). Reproduced with permission of Bloodaxe Books; **Drinkwater, John:** 'Moonlit Apples' by John Drinkwater. Used with permission of the author; **Duffy, Carol Ann:** 'The Duke of Fire and the Duchess of Ice' from *New and Collected Poems For Children* by Carol Ann Duffy (Faber, 2014). Copyright © Carol Ann Duffy. Reproduced by permission of the author c/o Rogers, Coleridge & White Ltd, 20 Powis Mews, London W11 1JN; **Farjeon, Eleanor:** 'Pencil and Paint', from *Blackbird Has Spoken* (Macmillan Children's Books, 1999). Published by permission of David Higham Associates on behalf of the estate of the author; **Frost, Robert,** 'Nothing Gold can Stay' and 'The Road Not Taken' from *The Poetry of Robert Frost*, (Jonathan Cape), reprinted by permission of The Random House Group Limited; **Giovanni, Nikki:** 'Winter Poem' from *My House* (HarperCollins, 1972). Copyright © Nikki Giovanni, renewed 2000. Reprinted by permission of HarperCollins Publishers; **Goodfellow, Matt:** 'Messages' by permission of the author; **Greenfield, Eloise:** 'Harriet Tubman' from *Honey, I Love and other love poems* (HarperCollins, 1986). Copyright © Eloise Greenfield, 1978. Used with permission of the publisher; **Hall, Ade:** 'Astrophysics Lesson' reproduced by permission of the author; **Harding, Mike:** 'Bomber's Moon', reproduced by permission of the author; **Harmer, David:** 'A Prayer for Lent' and 'Divali' reproduced by permission of the author; **Heaney, Seamus:** 'St Francis and the Birds' from *New and Selected Poems 1966–1987* by Seamus Heaney (Faber and Faber Ltd). 'The Railway Children' from *Wintering Out* (Faber & Faber Ltd, 2002) copyright © Seamus Heaney, 1972. 'Digging' from *New Selected Poems* (Faber & Faber Ltd, 2002) copyright © Seamus Heaney. All poems reproduced by permission of Faber & Faber Ltd; **Hegley, John:** 'Owl Poem' from *I Am a Poetato* by John Hegley (Frances Lincoln, 2013). Copyright © 2013. Reproduced by permission of Frances Lincoln Ltd; **Hughes, Ted:** 'Full Moon and Little Frieda' and 'Leaves' from *Collected Poems for Children* by Ted Hughes (Faber and Faber Ltd). All poems published by permission of Faber and Faber Ltd; **Kay, Jackie:** 'Fiere Good Nicht' from *Fiere* by Jackie Kay (Picador, 2011). Copyright © Jackie Kay. Used with permission of the publisher; **Lucie-Smith, Edward:** 'The Lesson' from *Changing Shape* by Edward Lucie-Smith (Carcanet Press Limited, 2002) copyright © Edward Lucie-Smith. Reproduced by permission of Carcanet Press Limited and by permission of the author c/o Rogers, Coleridge & White Ltd, 20

Powis Mews, London, W11 1JN; **MacLeish, Archibald:** 'Ars Poetica' from *Collected Poems 1917–1982* by Archibald MacLeish. Copyright © 1985 by The Estate of Archibald MacLeish. Reprinted by permission of Houghton Mifflin Harcourt Publishing Company. All rights reserved; **McGough, Roger:** 'The Leader' from *All the Best: The Selected Poems of Roger McGough* (Puffin, 2004) copyright © Roger McGough. All poems reprinted by permission of Penguin Random House; **Merriam, Eve:** 'Thumbprint' from *A Sky Full of Poems* by Eve Merriam copyright © 1964, 1970, 1973, 1986 Eve Merriam. Used by permission of the author; **Milne, A. A.,** 'Solitude' from *Now We Are Six* by A. A. Milne. Text copyright © The Trustees of the Pooh Properties 1927. Published by Egmont UK Ltd and used with permission; **Morgan, Edwin:** 'The Mummy' and 'The First Men on Mercury' from *Collected Poems* by Edwin Morgan (Carcanet Press Limited, 1990) copyright © Edwin Morgan. Reproduced by permission of Carcanet Press Limited; **Morgan, Michaela:** 'Malala' and 'My First Day at School' first published in *Reaching for the Stars* © Macmillan Children's Books 2017; **Moss, Jeff:** 'The Other Side of the Door' from *The Other Side of the Door* by Jeff Moss (Bantam Press, 1991). Copyright Jeff Moss. Used with permission of the publisher and the author; **Nesbitt, Kenn:** 'Xbox, Xbox – A Love Poem' copyright © 2013 Kenn Nesbitt. All Rights Reserved. Reprinted by permission of the author; **Noyes, Alfred**: 'from *The Highwayman*' by permission of The Society of Authors as the Literary Representative of the Estate of Alfred Noyes; **Oliver, Mary:** 'Wild Geese' from Dream Work by Mary Oliver, published by Grove Press, 1994, copyright © Mary Oliver. Reproduced by permission of Grove Atlantic, Inc., New York. Reproduced by permission of the the the Charlotte Sheedy Literary Agency, Inc; **Owen, Gareth:** 'Sports Report' copyright © Gareth Owen. Reproduced by permission of the author c/o Rogers, Coleridge & White Ltd, 20 Powis Mews, London, W11 1JN; **Patten, Brian:** 'Reading the Classics' and 'Not Only' from *Juggling With Gerbils* by Brian Patten. Published by Puffin, 2000. Copyright © Brian Patten. Reproduced by permission of the author c/o Rogers, Coleridge & White Ltd, 20 Powis Mews, London, W11 1JN; **Plath, Sylvia,** 'The Pheasant' from *Collected Poems* by Sylvia Plath (Faber and Faber Ltd) published by permission of Faber and Faber Ltd; **Prelutsky, Jack:** 'Today Is Very Boring' from *The New Kid on the Block* (Greenwillow Books, 1984) copyright © Jack Prelutsky, 1984; **Read, Herbert:** 'Aeroplanes' from *Selected Poetry* (Sinclair-Stevenson) published by permission of David Higham Associates on behalf of the estate of the author; **Rooney, Rachel:** 'Barrier' and 'Birthday' copyright © Rachel Rooney. reproduced by permission of the author; **Rosen, Michael:** 'Thirty Days Hath September' reproduced by permission of The Peters Fraser and Dunlop Group Ltd on behalf of the author; **Ryan, Kay:** 'Spiderweb' by Kay Ryan. Reprinted with permission of the publisher and the author; **Sandburg, Carl:** 'Who Do You Think You Are' and 'Arithmetic' from *The Complete Poems of Carl Sandburg*, Revised and

Expanded Edition. Copyright ©1970, 1969 by Lillian Steichen Sandburg, Trustee. Reprinted by permission of Houghton Mifflin Harcourt Publishing Company. All rights reserved; **Sassoon, Siegfried:** 'Does It Matter?' copyright Siegfried Sassoon by kind permission of the Estate of George Sassoon; **Smith, Stevie:** 'Not Waving but Drowning' from *Collected Poems and Drawings* by Stevie Smith (Faber and Faber Ltd). All poems published by permission of Faber and Faber Ltd; **Thomas, Dylan:** 'Do Not Go Gentle into that Good Night' from *The Collected Poems of Dylan Thomas: The Centenary Edition* (Weidenfeld & Nicholson) All poems published by permission of David Higham Associates on behalf of the estate of the author; **Walcott, Derek,** 'Love After Love' from *The Poetry of Derek Walcott 1948–2013* (Faber & Faber Ltd, 2014) copyright © Derek Walcott 1976. Reproduced by permission of Faber & Faber Ltd; **Williams, William Carlos**: 'The Red Wheelbarrow' from *Collected Poems Vol. 1 1909–1939* by William Carlos Williams (Carcanet Press Limited) published by permission of Carcanet Press Limited; **Williams, Hugo:** 'Joy' from *Collected Poems* (Faber & Faber Ltd, 2002) copyright © Hugo Williams, 2002. Reproduced by permission of Faber & Faber Ltd; **Wise Brown, Margaret:** 'The Secret Song' from *A Celebration of the Seasons: Goodnight Songs* (Sterling Publishing, 2015). Copyright © Margaret Wise Brown. Used with permission of the publisher.

Every effort has been made to trace the copyright holders, but if any have been inadvertently overlooked the publisher will be pleased to make the necessary arrangement at the first opportunity.